NICETOMEETYOUTOO!
VISUAL GREETINGS FROM BUSINESS CARDS TO IDENTITY PACKAGES

NICETOMEETYOUTOO!

First published and distributed by
viction:workshop ltd.

viction:ary™

Unit C, 7th Floor, Seabright Plaza,
9-23 Shell Street, North Point, Hong Kong
URL: www.victionary.com
Email: we@victionary.com

Edited and produced by viction:workshop ltd.

Book design by viction:workshop ltd.
Concepts & art direction by Victor Cheung

©2010 viction:workshop ltd.
The copyright on the individual text and
design work is held by the respective designers and contributors.

ISBN 978-988-17327-8-1

Printed and bound in China

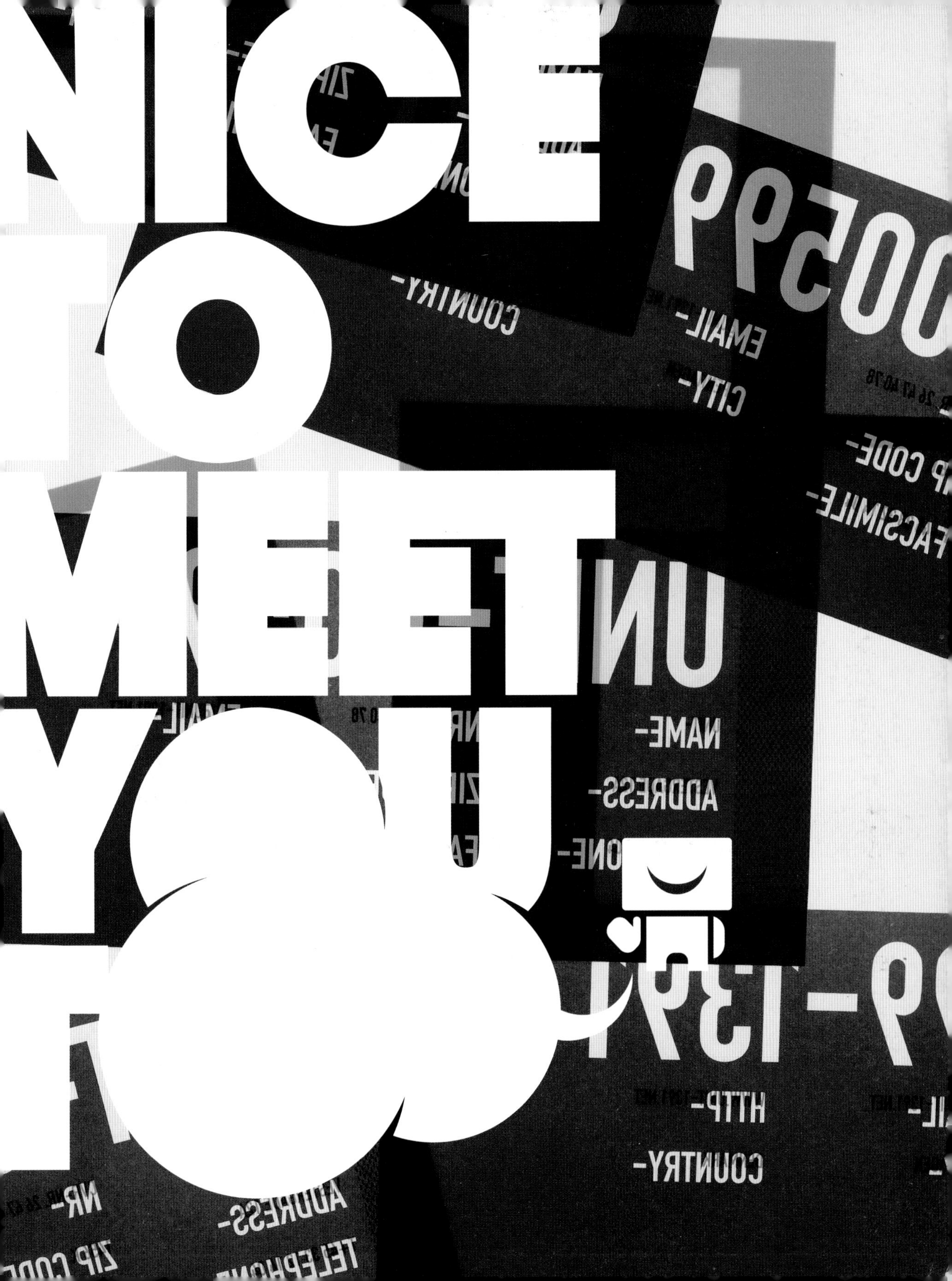
NICE
TO
MEET
YOU

Identity is what makes a person or company difference from another. It could be a name, their features in the first place, and slowly you will grow deeper to learn about their beliefs and the way they think and speak, putting together an image that requires observation, time and experience to build. From the business perspective, identity concludes the necessary values and tastes that a particular company could deliver via its products and services. And to customers, it helps them to distinguish you from a crowd when they need to make a choice. A well-executed identity design would greet your prospective clients the moment they look at it, where the less successful ones would simply look invisible among the excellent others. Without this visual wrap, a cheese will be just the dairy product that can fill your stomach; a designer will be someone with a hand to draw. It applies to businesses big and small, non-profit organisations, as well as individuals who have talents to show.

Business card is one convenient tool to display your identity. Light and small to carry and inexpensive to produce in quantity, it makes a perfect, concrete summary about your expertise and experience. It provides a good starting point to greet others and introduce yourself in many occasions and to many at a time. Be it a card by itself or a part of a complete identity project, the card acts an epitome of your business and you yourself. It speaks for you when you are not there. If it functions well, it could add creditability and win confidence before the users talk to you in person. It helps you to connect people, extend your network and spread your name in a quick and easy way, just like why reporters need to exchange cards and plumbers leave their cards behind in the neighbourhood's mailboxes from time to time.

The course of developing an efficient business card is never an easy undertaking despite the ready availability and variety of advanced printing technology and printable media. Personality would be the key thing that designers need to work on beyond that minimal information you need to show on the card. Whether a custom typeface is unique enough to conclude the essense of a business, like INADA GUMI (P. 060) by COMMUNE; if everything should start from a logo design that could function alone or expand to yield powerful supergraphics to dress up the entire store like L'escalier identity (P. 102) by &Larry; or an unorthodox approach could meet the expectations of cheese lovers, like the black-and-white identity for boutique cheese company, Over The Moon Dairy (P. 016) also by &Larry — these are all results of thorough communication between designers and clients when it comes to commissions, or rigorous self-analyses for self-promotion works.

There are many ways to say the same thing, and even the same font or material could tell a very different story behind the owners and the designs. Today's young designers have made their ways to construct meanings with the brilliant use of graphics and familiar techniques. You will see how A Friend Of Mine Design Studio (P. 163) demonstrates their attitude towards commissions and fun via simple colour combinations; how figurative formats could effectively bring forward the name and editorial directions of a publication, like bracket (P. 216) by SILNT; how some people would dare to let the words slip out of their mouths, like what Megan Cummins did in her cards (P. 027). And, while some tend to speak an easy language, like Trapped in Suburbia (P. 188) putting their practice into actual words for you to read out loud, some engage you with the challenge to be patience, like 'another bloomin' designer' (P. 220) by Jamie Wieck who invite you to soak his card with water and wait for a miniature houseplant to grow. For attempts that go beyond the flat surface and involve a third medium, see how Rice 5 pique you curiosity with the chemical reaction between your webcam, a simple code and augmented reality technology common in virtual games and website design (P. 161).

There are so many different business card solutions out there, but it's not difficult to tell why some unusual cards get noticed, and which one gives a good and lovely taste. Like how Jordan Metcalf, who took the sophisticate shape of triangular planes hand-cut to manifest his love and honour the subject of art and good design (P. 006), or the special features of 'Pachica', a special Japanese paper inspired the design of PataPri (P. 101) by Yuko Uemura in return. And as when the discussion on sustaining our precious environment remains hot, on how we could minimise pollution to the Earth and make better use of resources available to hand, you will find a resourceful showcase of environmentally-friendly solutions, ranging from the choices of green inks in use, recycle paper, remnants of materials from earlier projects, or invite users to extend the life span of the items they could get.

Witnessing how business cards have evolved to make memories and impress in this over-communicated society, this book is set to discover how designers have expanded the capacity and functions of this every day stationery beyond its restricted dimensions and weight. With a comprehensive collection of business cards and identity designs, where some demonstrate an evolution in brand values based on an existing identity and some done in a flash of time to fit a tight budget or quick deadline, Nice to Meet You Too tells you how today's business cards compose a simple yet powerful message in a nutshell.

001

Jordan Metcalf

CL: Jordan Metcalf
BN: Graphic Designer, Illustrator
DE: Jordan Metcalf

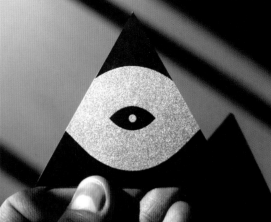

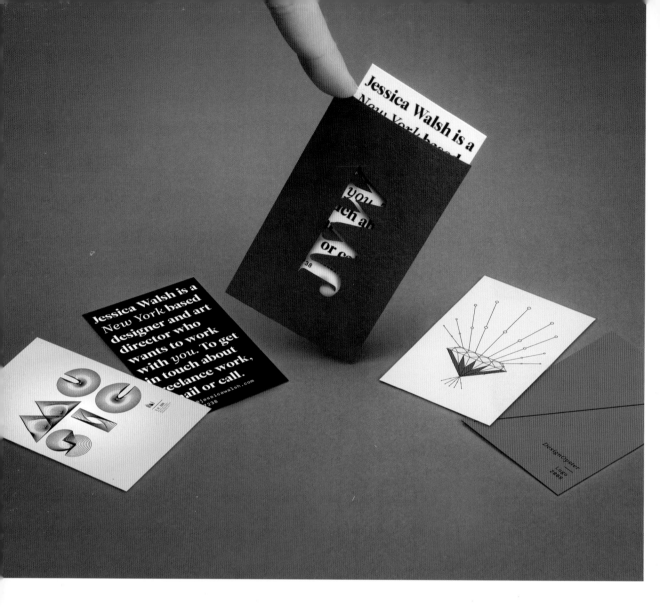

002
―――

Jessica Walsh

CL: Jessica Walsh
BN: Graphic designer, Illustrator
DE: Jessica Walsh

MUR Arquitectos/Arkitektar Identity

CL: MUR Arquitectos/Arkitektar
BN: Architecture and interior design firm
DE: GSA Design

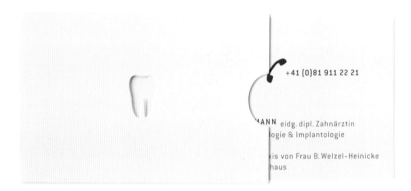

MANN eidg. dipl. Zahnärztin
logie & Implantologie

xis von Frau B. Welzel-Heinicke
haus

 +41 (0)81 911 22 21

DR. ANITA WEHRLE LECHMANN eidg. dipl. Zahnärztin
Spezialausbildung in Parodontologie & Implantologie
contact@dentista-surselva.ch
Behandlung in der Zahnarztpraxis von Frau B. Welzel-Heinicke
Promenada 39, 7018 Flims Waldhaus

004
___

Dr. Anita Wehlre-Lechmann

CL: Dr. Anita Wehlre-Lechmann
BN: Dentist
DE: Remo Caminada

jungeschachtel

CL: jungeschachtel
    BN: Design firm
DE: jungeschachtel

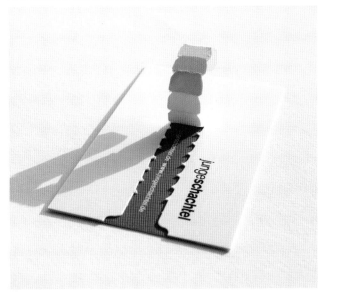

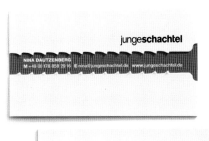

Montreux Jazz Café

CL: Montreux Jazz Café
BN: Café
DE: Schaffter Sahli

Photography: Olivier Pasqual

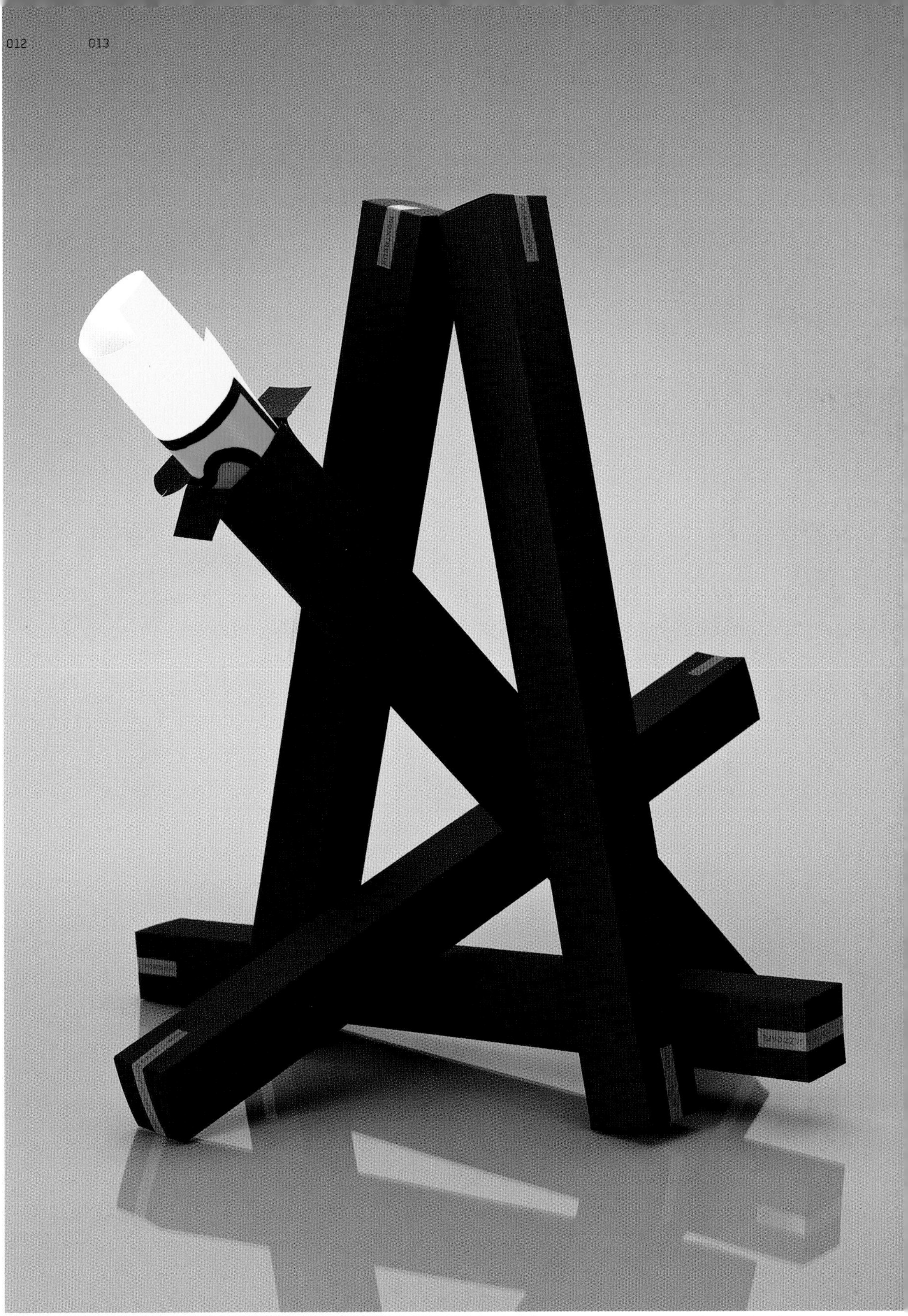

Photography: Olivier Pasqual

007

Kaffe

CL: Kaffe (College project)
BN: Coffee Shop
DE: Felix Lobelius

Over The Moon Dairy

CL: Over The Moon Dairy Co.
BN: Cheese boutique
DE: The Creative Method

GSA DESIGN

Rua Guilherme Costa Carvalho, 25 1º S3, 4000-274 Porto, Portugal /
T +351 220 174 629 / info@gsadesign.net / www.gsadesign.net

009
—

Raspadinha (Scratch n' win)

CL: GSA Design
BN: Graphic design collective
DE: GSA Design

Dancemade 2006

CL: dancemade
BN: Graphic designer
DE: Jens Nilsson

Kinokuniya

CL: Kinokuniya (College project)
BN: Bookshop
DE: Felix Lobelius

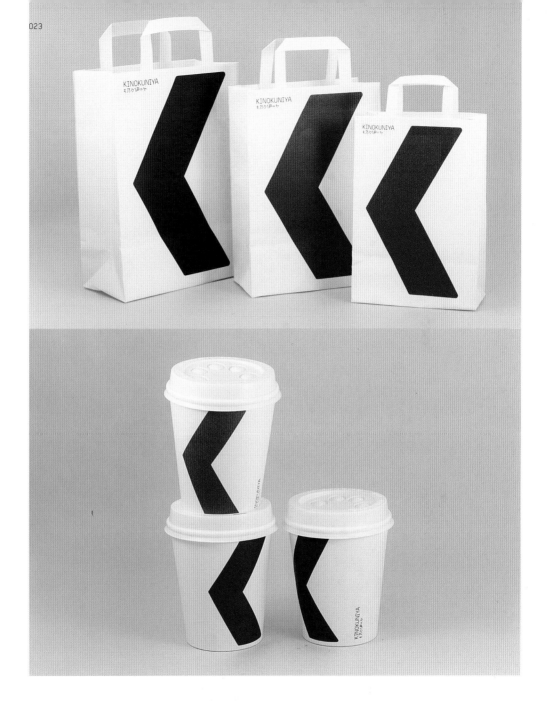

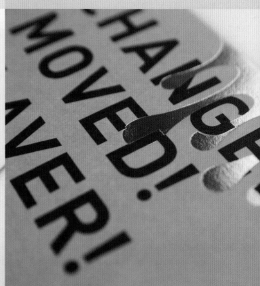

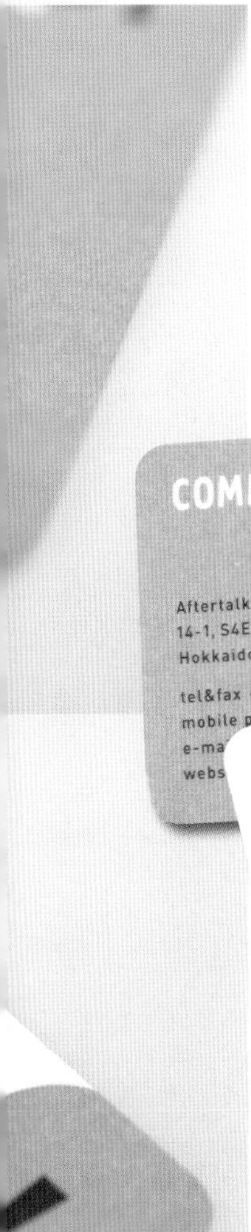

WE CHANGED!
WE MOVED!
E SLAVER!

COMMUNE®

RYO UEDA
Art Director, Designer

Aftertalk bld. 2F
14-1, S4E3, Chuo-ku, Sappro
Hokkaido 060-0054 Japan

tel&fax +81 11 807 8035
mobile phon
e-ma
webs

上田 亮
Art Director, Designer

COMMUNE®

060 0054
札幌市中央区南4条東3丁目14-1
aftertalk bld. 2F

tel&fax 011 807 8035
mobile phone 090 7651 6648
e-mail ryo-ueda@commune-inc.jp
website www.commune-inc.jp

Chuo-ku, Sappro
Japan

COMMUNE®

012

We changed! We moved! We slaver!

CL: COMMUNE
BN: Graphic design firm
DE: COMMUNE

Sarah Davies

CL: Sarah Davies
BN: TV presenter, Model
DE: Couple

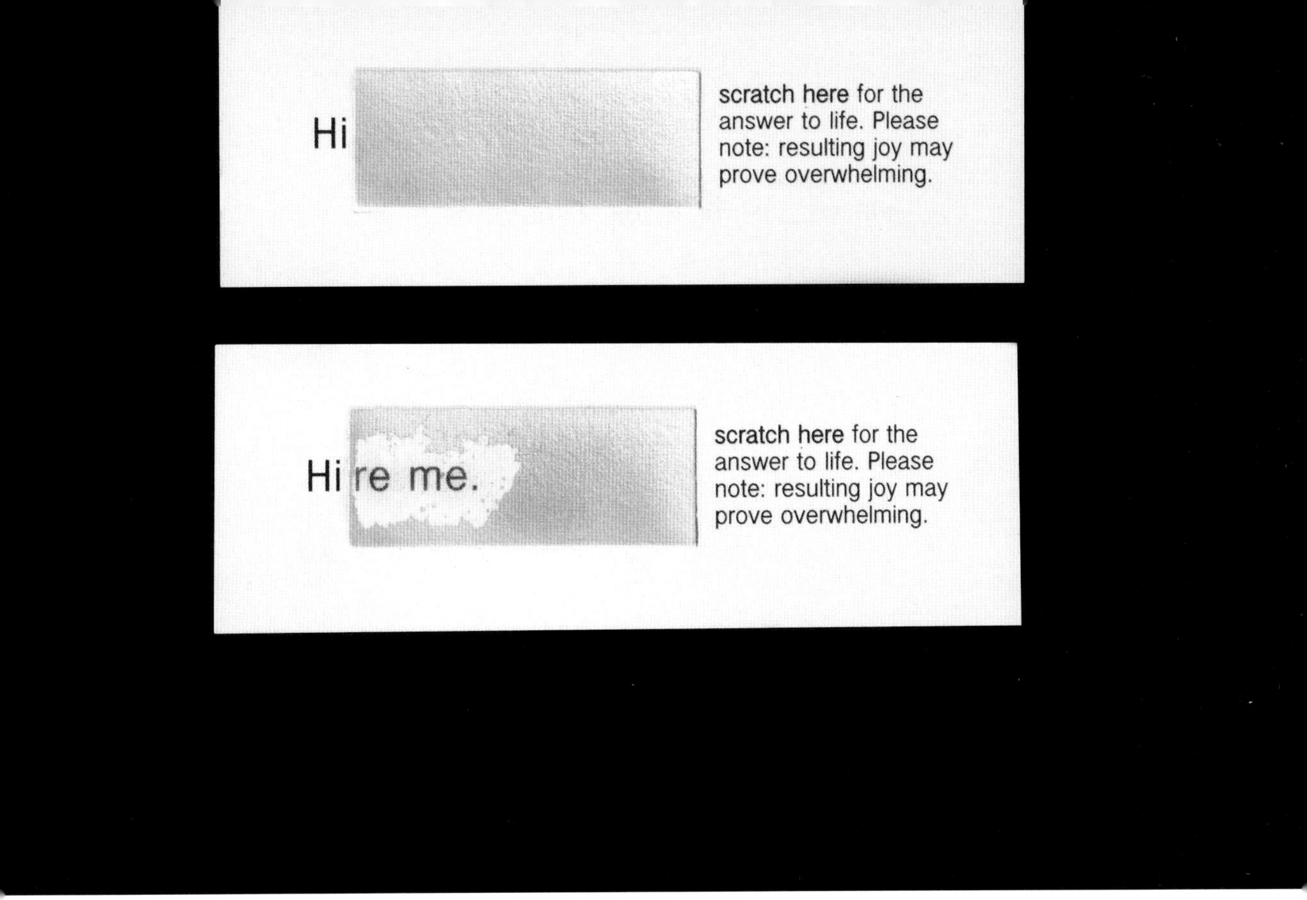

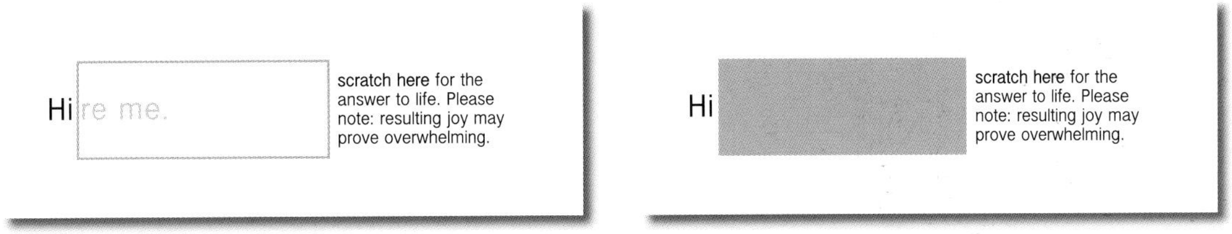

Hi[ ] **scratch here** for the answer to life. Please note: resulting joy may prove overwhelming.

Hi re me. **scratch here** for the answer to life. Please note: resulting joy may prove overwhelming.

Hi re me. scratch here for the answer to life. Please note: resulting joy may prove overwhelming.

Hi [ ] scratch here for the answer to life. Please note: resulting joy may prove overwhelming.

Megan Cummins

graphic designer www.megancummins.com call 901.485.9428 e-mail cumminsdesign@gmail.com

014

Megan Cummins

CL: Megan Cummins
BN: Graphic designer
DE: Megan Cummins

015
━━━

Arch Idea Identity

CL: Arch Idea Ltd.
BN: Architecture firm
DE: Transformer studio

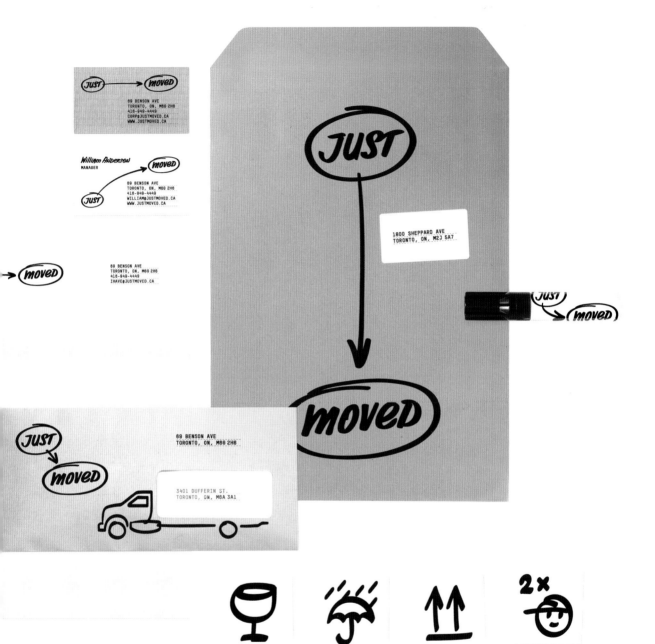

016

Just Moved Identity

CL: Just Moved Ltd.
BN: Residential moving company
DE: Transformer studio

017

———

Call me for a new haircut

CL: Demian Conrad Design
BN: Graphic and industrial designer
DE: Demian Conrad Design

Card composer

CL: Frank Salis
CL: Jazz musician, Composer
DE: Demian Conrad Design

YZ International

CL: YZ International
BN: Artist agency
DE: Form+Format

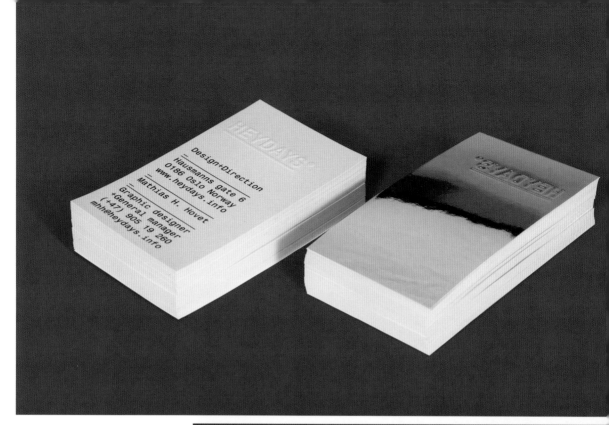

Heydays Stationery

CL: Heydays
BN: Design firm
DE: Heydays

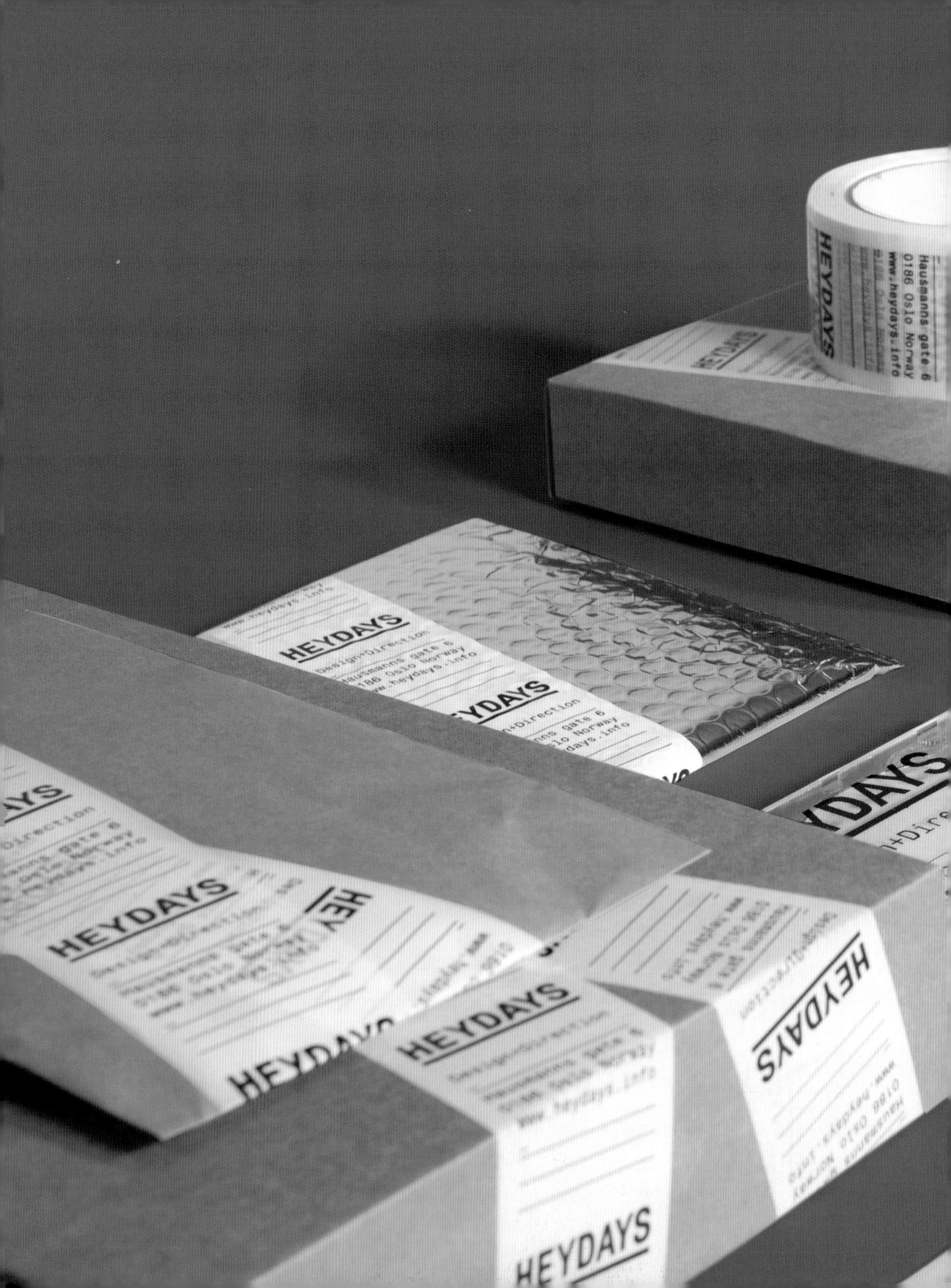
HEYDAYS
Hausmanns gate 6
0186 Oslo Norway
www.heydays.info
HEYDAYS
Design+Direction
Hausmanns gate 6
0186 Oslo Norway
www.heydays.info

021

Stella Filante

CL: Stella Filante
BN: Boutique
DE: paperwhite studio

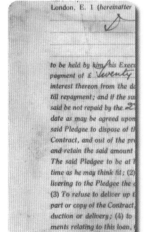

THE PAWN

CL: THE PAWN
BN: Gastropub
DE: C plus C Workshop Ltd.

beautiful

Everything has its beauty, but not everyone sees it.

Roy Poh - Creative Director
Call (65) 9767 2355
Fax (65) 6348 6077
roy@abeautifuldesign.com.sg
www.abeautifuldesign.com.sg

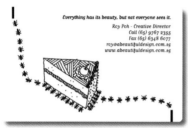

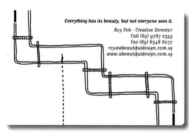

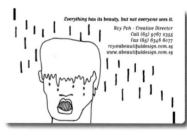

023

Beautiful CI

CL: Beautiful
BN: Graphic design firm
DE: Beautiful

m 852 9880 1210
e 0001a84000.com.hk
t 852 2887 1321
f 852 2503 1321
217 innocentre 72 tat chee avenue
kowloon tong hongkong
www.84000.com.hk

84000communications
stanley wong

m 852 9880 1210
e 0001a84000.com.hk
t 852 2887 1321
f 852 2503 1321
217 innocentre 72 tat chee avenue
kowloon tong hongkong
www.84000.com.hk

024

Infinite possibility

CL: 84000 communications
BN: Marketing and communication agency
DE: 84000 communications

NR1391

CL: UNIT-
BN: Graphic design collective
DE: UNIT-

UNIT-00629-1391

WWW.UNIT-1391.NET

NFO@UNIT-1391.NET

DENMARK

CVR-NR. 26 47 40 78

COPENHAGEN

1456 K

RGADE 12A

F+45 33 32 14 04

5 33 12 14 04

UNIT-01155-1391

PRODUCT #
CLIENT #
CASE #
CONTENT
DATE

EMAIL-
NR-
NAME-
CITY-
ZIP CODE-
ADDRESS-
FACSIMILE-
TELEPHONE-

Eighteen Percent

CL: Eighteen Percent
BN: Analogue and digital photography
DE: Tiana Vasiljev

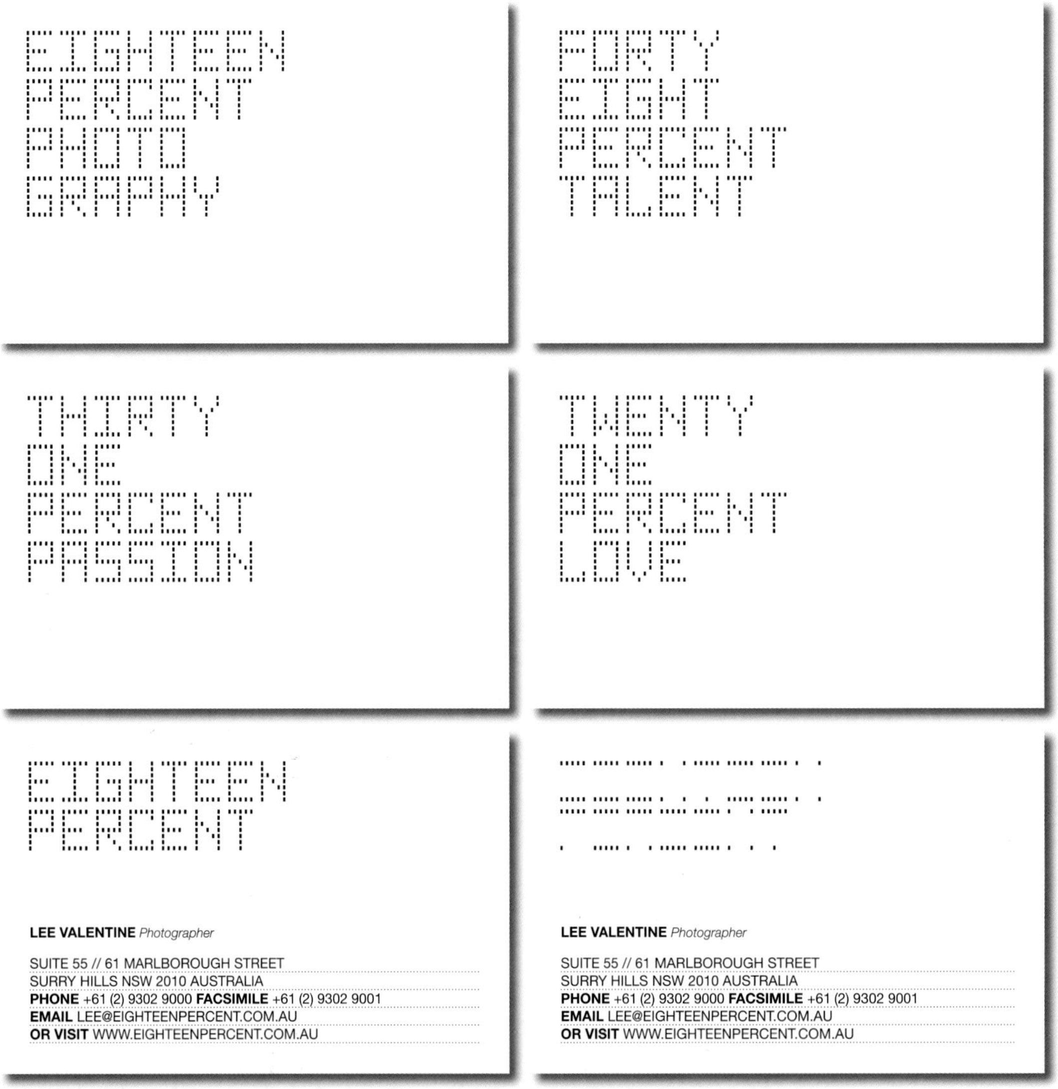

EIGHTEEN
PERCENT
PHOTO
GRAPHY

FORTY
EIGHT
PERCENT
TALENT

THIRTY
ONE
PERCENT
PASSION

TWENTY
ONE
PERCENT
LOVE

EIGHTEEN
PERCENT

LEE VALENTINE *Photographer*

SUITE 55 // 61 MARLBOROUGH STREET
SURRY HILLS NSW 2010 AUSTRALIA
PHONE +61 (2) 9302 9000 **FACSIMILE** +61 (2) 9302 9001
EMAIL LEE@EIGHTEENPERCENT.COM.AU
OR VISIT WWW.EIGHTEENPERCENT.COM.AU

LEE VALENTINE *Photographer*

SUITE 55 // 61 MARLBOROUGH STREET
SURRY HILLS NSW 2010 AUSTRALIA
PHONE +61 (2) 9302 9000 **FACSIMILE** +61 (2) 9302 9001
EMAIL LEE@EIGHTEENPERCENT.COM.AU
OR VISIT WWW.EIGHTEENPERCENT.COM.AU

ESTUDIO

CL: ESTUDIO
BN: Photography studio
DE: C plus C Workshop Ltd.

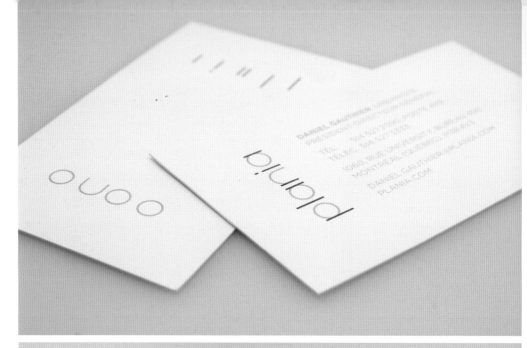

Plania

CL: Plania
BN: Urban planning company
DE: Ryan Crouchman, Bleublancrouge

029

Dreams Factory

CL: Dreams Factory
BN: Photography studio
DE: Driv Loo

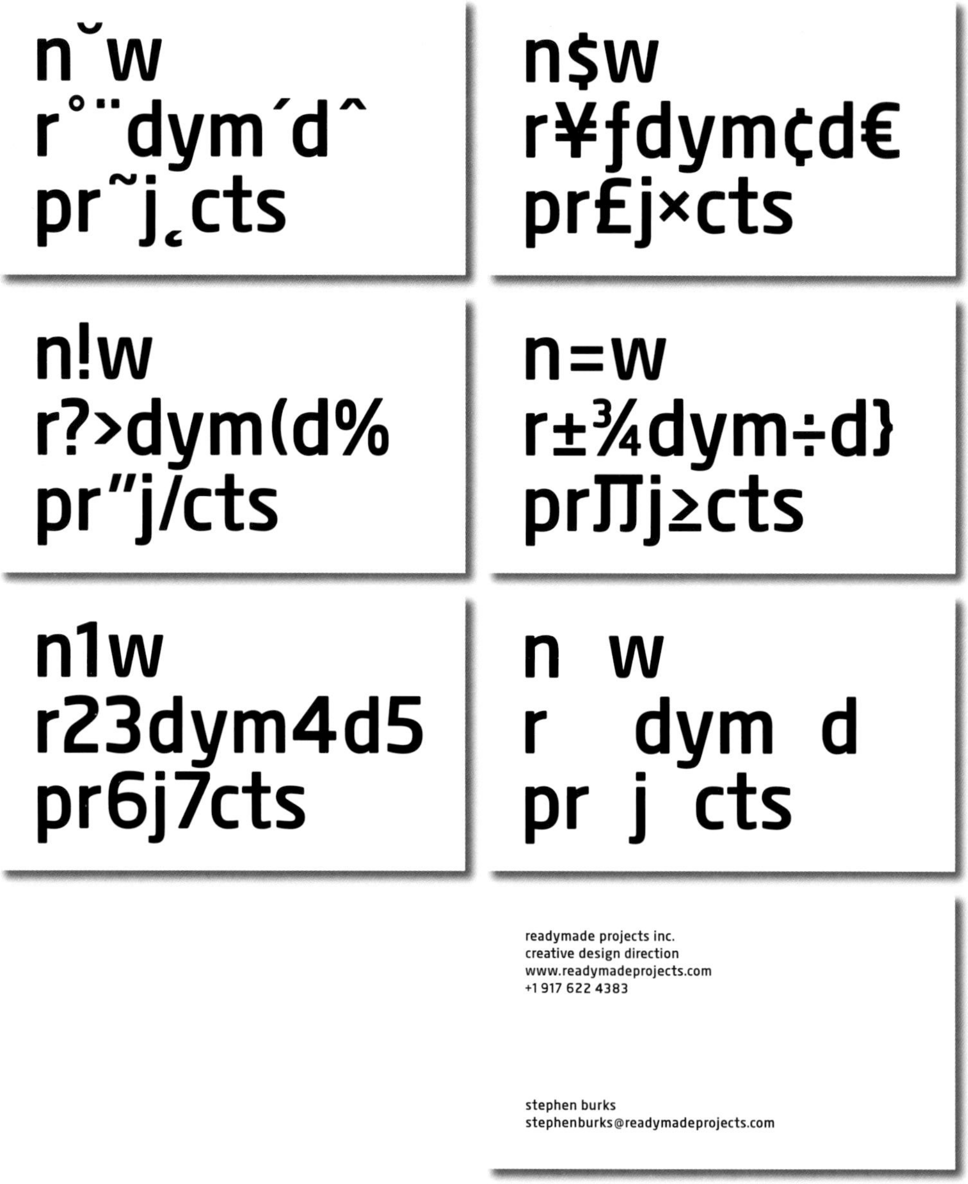

nˇw
r°¨dym´d^
pr~j¸cts

n$w
r¥ʃdym¢d€
pr£j×cts

n!w
r?>dym(d%
pr"j/cts

n=w
r±¾dym÷d}
prЛj≥cts

n1w
r23dym4d5
pr6j7cts

n w
r dym d
pr j cts

readymade projects inc.
creative design direction
www.readymadeprojects.com
+1 917 622 4383

stephen burks
stephenburks@readymadeprojects.com

New Readymade Projects identity

CL: New Readymade Projects
BN: Industrial designer
DE: Studio Lin

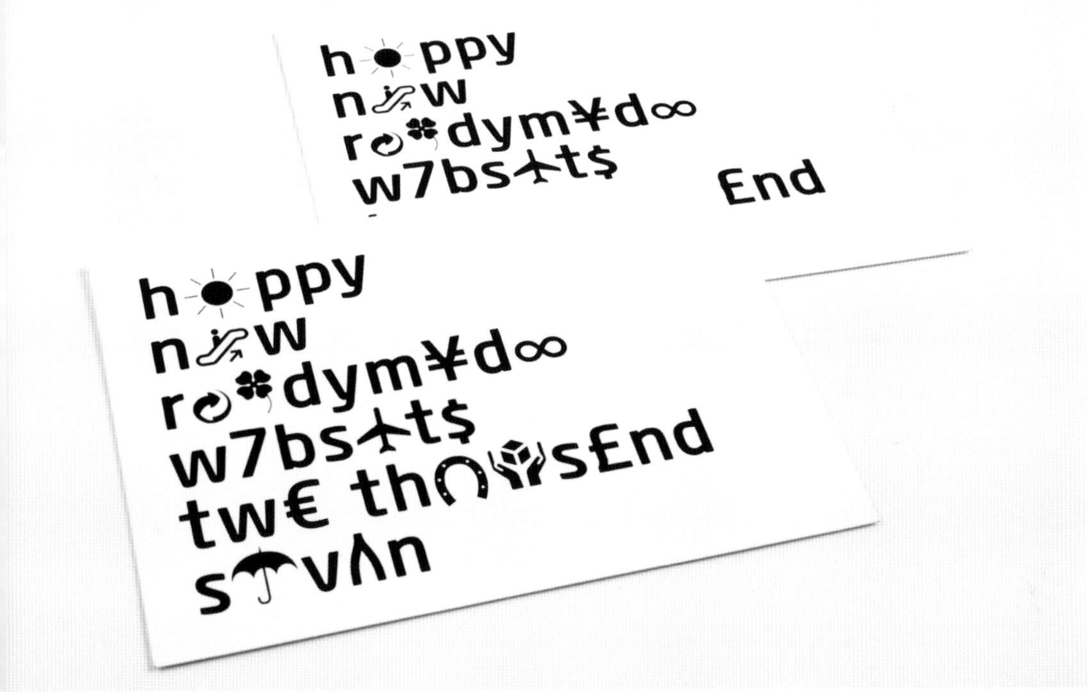

h☀ppy
n🦎w
r☘dym¥d∞
w7bs✈t$ End

h☀ppy
n🦎w
r☘dym¥d∞
w7bs✈t$
tw€ th🙌sEnd
s☂v∧n

n˘˘w
r°˙˙dym´d¯
pr˜j˙cts

n1w
r23dym4d5
pr6ij/cts

n1w
r½>dym¢d%
pr⅛j˙cts

n˙w
r¥fdym¢d€
prЄj×cts

n=w
r±¾dym=d)
prⅢj×cts

n˙w
r°˙˙dym´d¯
pr˜j˙cts

n˘w
r°˙˙dym´d¯
pr˜j˙cts

n$w
r¥fdym¢d€
prЄj×cts

readymade projects inc.
creative design direction
www.readymade-projects.com
451 greenwich street
studio 506 new york ny 10013
+1 917 622 4383

031

Periodus Coaster

CL: Antrepo Design Industry
BN: Design firm
DE: Antrepo Design Industry

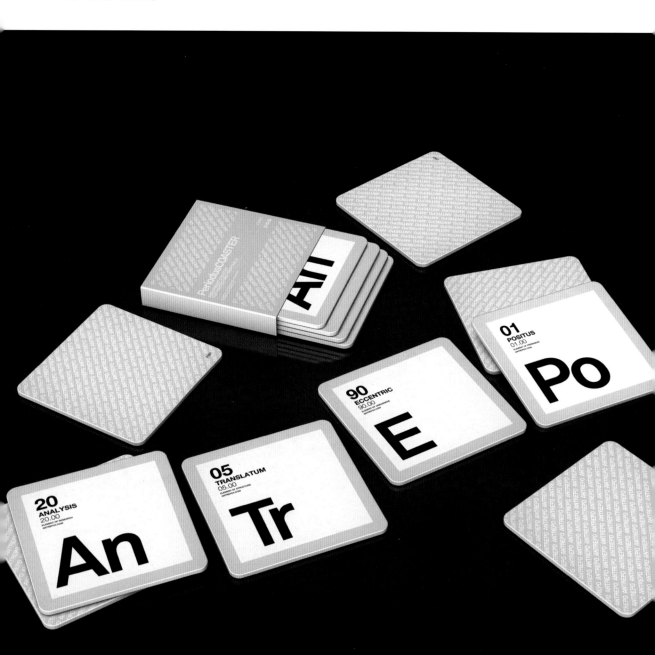

032

Daniel Calabro

CL: Daniel Calabro
BN: Guitar teacher
DE: 21-19

033

Chuan Pictures identity

CL: Chuan Pictures
BN: Production company
DE: &Larry

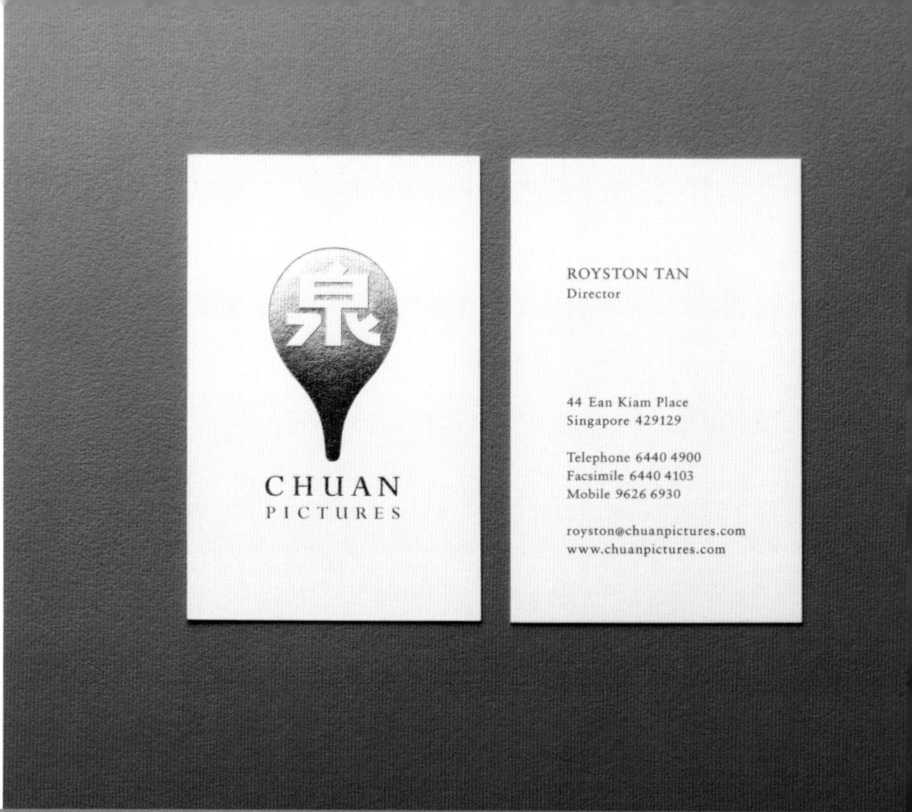

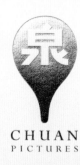

泉
CHUAN
PICTURES
ROYSTON TAN
Director
44 Ean Kiam Place
Singapore 429129
Telephone 6440 4900
Facsimile 6440 4103
Mobile 9626 6930
royston@chuanpictures.com
www.chuanpictures.com

泉
CHUAN
PICTURES
44 Ean Kiam Place
Singapore 429129
Telephone 6440 4900
Facsimile 6440 4103
www.chuanpictures.com

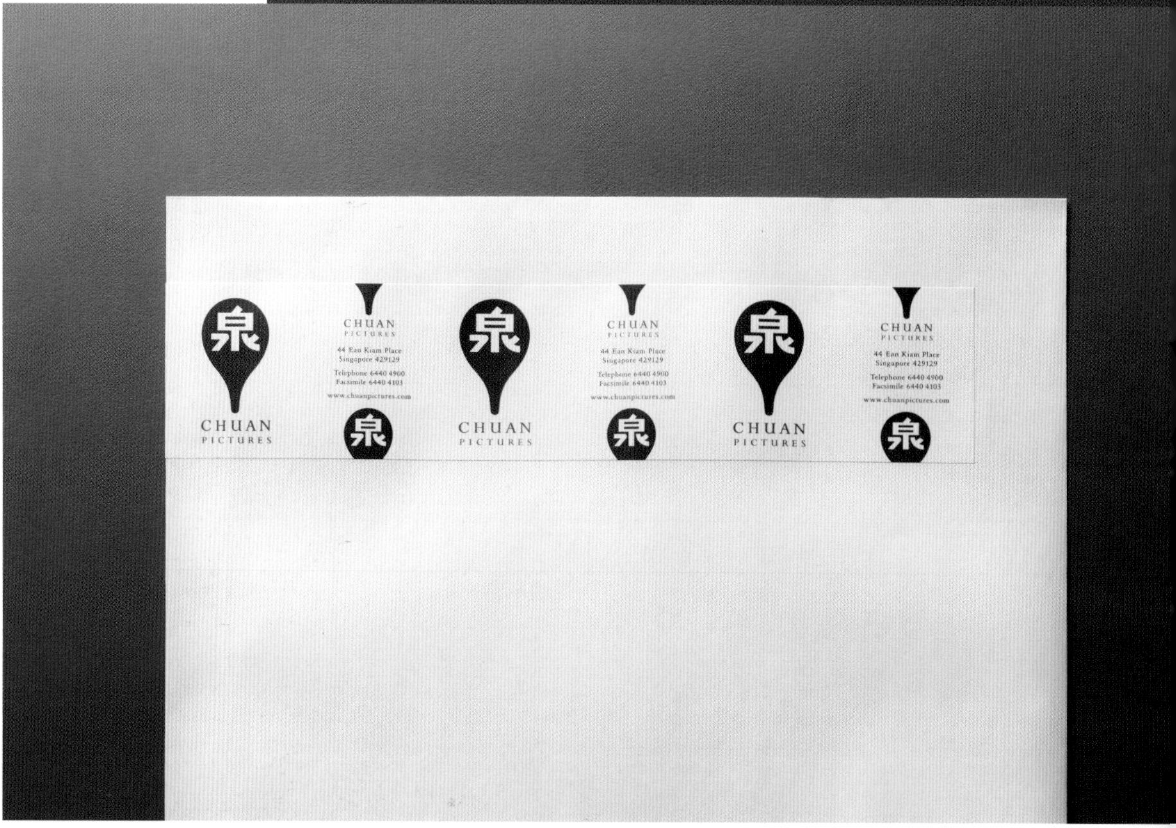

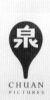

GIA identity

CL: General Insurance
Association of Singapore
BN: Professional association
DE: &Larry

035

INADA GUMI

CL: INADA GUMI
BN: Theatrical team
DE: COMMUNE

A-TO

CL: A-TO
BN: Arts and crafts shop
DE: COMMUNE

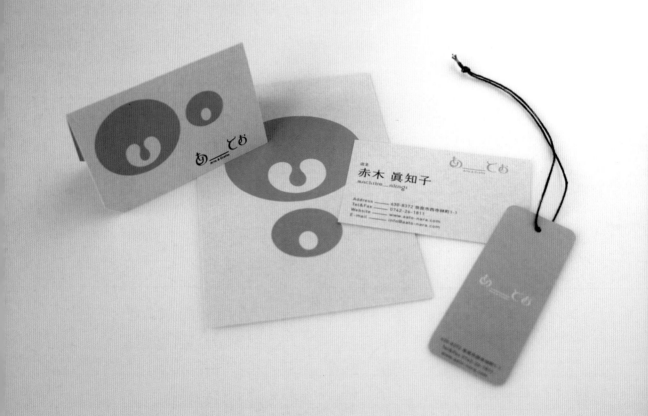

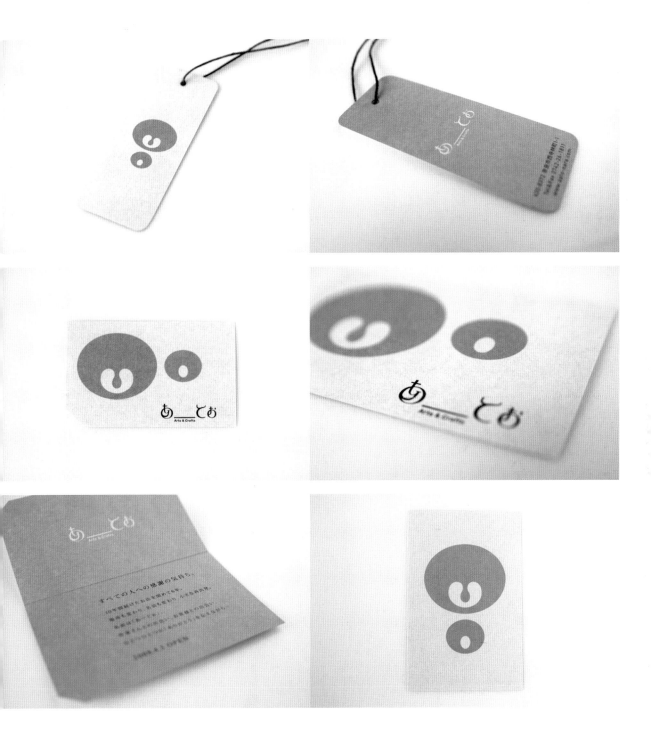

PLAYZEBRA MAGAZINE
VIA VERDI 12 10124 **TORINO**
T/F {PLUS}39 011 8136068
CANNAREGIO 1226 30121 **VENEZIA**
T {PLUS} 39 041 0994897
WWW{DOT}PLAYZEBRA{DOT}IT
LOOK{AT}PLAYZEBRA{DOT}IT

NELLO ~~ANNA PAOLO SARAH BEPPE ANDREA OTTO STENECH~~
~~RIELLO~~ RUSSO ~~DEWILDE TAMBOSCO FOLLO VACCARIELLO~~
M {PLUS}39 ~~333 8556521~~ 347 0560197 ~~328 5350193~~
~~347 6281960 349 5209941 338 4502745~~
E ~~PAOLO SARAH OTTO~~ NELLO ~~ANNA BEPPE ANDREA~~
{AT}PLAYZEBRA{DOT}IT

Playzebra Magazine

CL: Playzebra Magazine
BN: Art and design magazine
DE: Nello Russo

PLAYZEBRA MAGAZINE
VIA VERDI 12 10124 **TORINO**
T/F {PLUS}39 011 8136068
CANNAREGIO 1226 30121 **VENEZIA**
T {PLUS} 39 041 0994897
WWW{DOT}PLAYZEBRA{DOT}IT
LOOK{AT}PLAYZEBRA{DOT}IT

NELLO ANNA PAOLO SARAH BEPPE DIEGO ANDREA OTTO
STENECH RIELLO RUSSO DEWILDE TAMBOSCO FOLLO
MORIONDO VACCARIELLO
MOBILE: {PLUS}39 333 8556521 347 0560197 328 5350193
347 0797681 347 9330732 347 6281960 349 5209941 338 4502745
E-MAIL: PAOLO SARAH OTTO NELLO ANNA DIEGO
BEPPE ANDREA {AT}PLAYZEBRA{DOT}IT

038

Anthony James Banks

CL: Anthony James Banks
BN: Consultant orthopaedic surgeon
DE: Face37

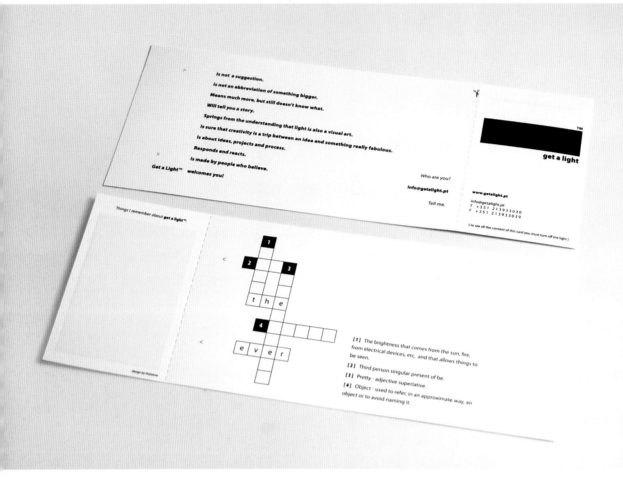

Is not a suggestion.

Is not an abbreviation of something bigger.

Means much more, but still doesn't know what.

Will tell you a story.

Springs from the understanding that light is also a visual art.

Is sure that creativity is a trip between an idea and something really fabulous.

Is about ideas, projects and process.

Responds and reacts.

Is made by people who believe.

Get a Light™ welcomes you!

Who are you?

info@getalight.pt

Tell me.

www.getalight.pt

info@getalight.pt
T +351 213933030
F +351 213933039

[to see all the content of this card you must turn off the light]

TM

get a light

Things I remember about **get a light**™:

[1] The brightness that comes from the sun, fire, from electrical devices, etc. and that allows things to be seen.

[2] Third person singular present of be.

[3] Pretty - adjective superlative.

[4] Object - used to refer, in an approximate way, an object or to avoid naming it.

design by thisislove

Hello, nice to meet you!

My name is **Margarida Eusébio** and I'm the Founder and Manager Partner of **get a light™**. My phone number is **+351 91 1010440** and my e-mail is **margarida@getalight.pt**.

light becomes architecture.

TM

get a light

www.getalight.pt

info@getalight.pt
T +351 21 3933030
F +351 21 3933039
LX Factory
Rua Rodrigues Faria 103
espaço G.02
1300-501 Lisboa_Portugal

[to see all the content of this card you must turn off the light]

Things I remember about **get a light**™:

039

get a light

CL: get a light
BN: Architecture and lighting design firm
DE: thisislove studio

Tallaght Community Arts identity

CL: Tallaght Community Arts
BN: Community arts organisation
DE: Aad

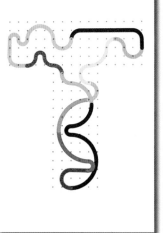

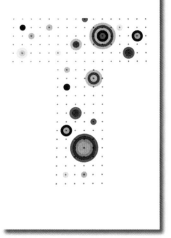

Tallaght Community Arts

Patricia Baker
Creative Producer / Arts

Unit 1   T +353 1 4621501
Village Square   F +353 1 4621640
Tallaght   info@tallaghtarts.ie
Dublin 24   www.tallaghtarts.ie

Tallaght Community Arts

Tony Fegan
Director

Unit 1   T +353 1 4621501
Village Square   F +353 1 4621640
Tallaght   info@tallaghtarts.ie
Dublin 24   www.tallaghtarts.ie

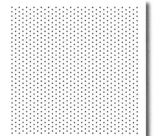

Kemistry Gallery

Alastair Coe {Gallery Manager}
alastair@kemistrygallery.co.uk

Gallery No: +44 (0)20 7729 3636
Mobile No: +44 (0)77 8525 1663
43 Charlotte Road, London EC2A 3PD
kemistrygallery.co.uk

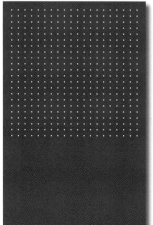

Kemistry Gallery

Alastair Coe {Gallery Manager}
alastair@kemistrygallery.co.uk

Gallery No: +44 (0)20 7729 3636
Mobile No: +44 (0)77 8525 1663
43 Charlotte Road, London EC2A 3PD
kemistrygallery.co.uk

Kemistry Gallery

43 Charlotte Road
London EC2A 3PD
+44 (0)20 7729 3636
info@kemistrygallery.co.uk
kemistrygallery.co.uk

Opening Hours:
Mon – Fri {10.00 – 18.00}
Sat {11.00 – 16.00}

Private View:
If you'd like to be invited to future
private viewings, contact us on
guestlist@kemistrygallery.co.uk

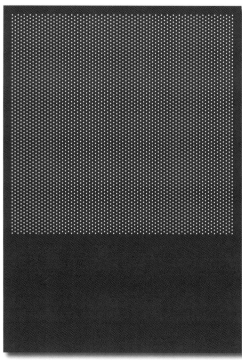

041
———

Kemistry Gallery stationery

CL: Kemistry Gallery
BN: Gallery
DE: Proud Creative

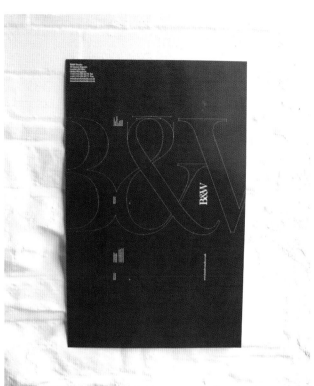

B&W Studio

CL: B&W Studio
BN: Graphic Design firm
DE: B&W Studio

Russell Marsh Casting

CL: Russell Marsh Casting
BN: Casting agency
DE: Mind Design

Name Surname
Casting Director

Russell Marsh Casting
110 Great Portland Street
London w1w 6pq
Telephone: +44 (0)20 7636 6316
Facsimile: +44 (0)20 7636 6356
Mobile: +44 (0)1234 567 890
name@russellmarshcasting.com

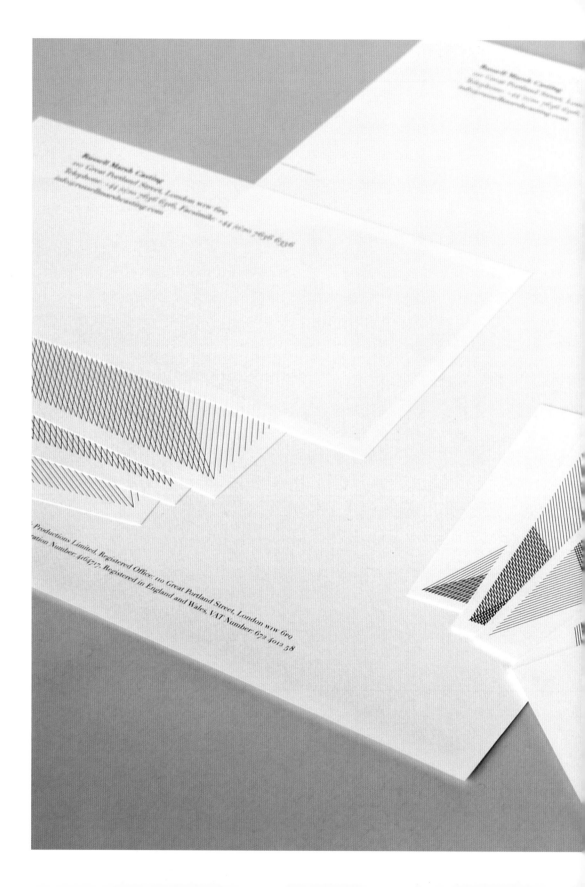

Russell Marsh
Casting Director
Russell Marsh Casting
110 Great Portland Street
London w1w 6ro
Telephone: +44 (0)20 7636 6316
Facsimile: +44 (0)20 7636 6356
Mobile: +44 (0)7768 007 321
russell@russellmarshcasting.com

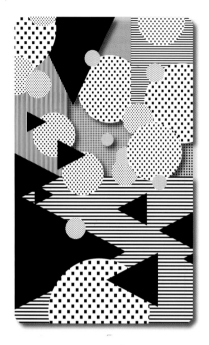

WITH COMPLIMENTS FROM
CLAIRE INCORRUPTIBLE
STYLING & EXCLUSIVE DRAPERY

CLAIREINC
.COM

WE HOPE YOU ♥

IF YOU HAVE ANY CONCERNS WITH
YOUR ORDER PLEASE EMAIL US
BELINDA@CLAIREINC.COM

CLAIRE INCORRUPTIBLE
STYLING & EXCLUSIVE DRAPERY

CLAIREINC
.COM

BELINDA HUMPHRIS
PH. +61 422 180 032
BELINDA@CLAIREINC.COM

044

Claire Inc identity

CL: Claire Inc
BN: Online fashion retailer
DE: Mash

CLAIRE INCORRUPTIBLE
STYLING & EXCLUSIVE DRAPERY

CLAIREINC
.COM

BELINDA HUMPHRIS
PH. +61 422 180 032
BELINDA@CLAIREINC.COM

WITH COMPLIMENTS FROM
CLAIRE INCORRUPTIBLE
STYLING & EXCLUSIVE DRAPERY

CLAIREINC
.COM

WE HOPE YOU ♥

IF YOU HAVE ANY CONCERNS WITH
YOUR ORDER PLEASE EMAIL US
BELINDA@CLAIREINC.COM

Eastside Bookshop identity

CL: Eastside Books LTD UK
BN: Bookshop
DE: Mihail Mihaylov

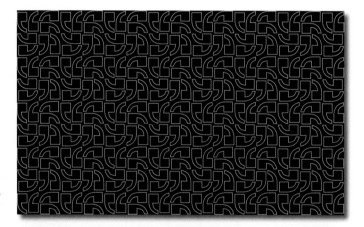

Kalina Dimitrova
Manager

Telephone: 020 7247 0216
Fax: 020 7377 6120
Email: info@eastsidebooks.co.uk
Web: www.eastsidebooks.co.uk

Paramount

CL: Paramount
BN: Members' club
DE: Mind Design, Tom Dixon

PARAMOUNT

NAME SURNAME
MOBILE: +44 (0)1234 567 890
DIRECT DIAL: +44 (0)12 3456 7890
EMAIL: name@paramount.uk.net

Centre Point
101–103 New Oxford Street
London WC1A 1DD
PHONE: +44 (0)20 7420 2900
FAX: +44 (0)20 7420 2919
EMAIL: info@paramount.uk.net
www.paramount.uk.net

The Lollipop Shoppe identity

CL: The Lollipop Shoppe
BN: Furniture and accessories
retailer
DE: StudioMakgill

WE
ARE
OPEN

Opening times
Monday—Saturday, 10am—6pm
Sunday, Closed
Phone +44 (0)1273 699119
www.thelollipopshoppe.co.uk

THE
LOLLIPOP
SHOPPE

Alan Valek

CL: Alan Valek
BN: Art director, Graphic designer
DE: Alan Valek

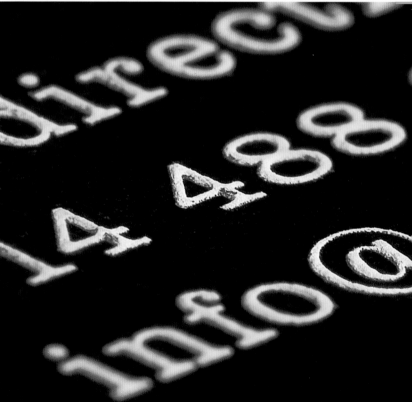

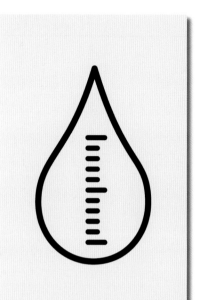

I+Drink

PABLO ALVAREZ
Director Financiero

e-mail: pabloalvarez@imasdrink.com
C: Fruela 3, 33007 Oviedo
T: +34 985 20 81 20
F: +34 985 20 81 40
W: www.imasdrink.com

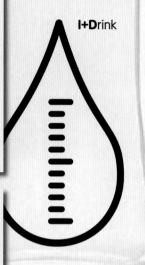

PABLO ALVAREZ
Director Financiero

e-mail: pabloalvarez@imasdrink.com
C: Fruela 3, 33007 Oviedo
T: +34 985 20 81 20
F: +34 985 20 81 40
W: www.imasdrink.com

049

I+Drink

CL: I+Drink
BN: Bar
DE: m Barcelona

I+Mo

I+Lov

I+Pois

I+Drink

I+D

I+Drink

I+Tennessee
I+Lemon
I+Bordeaux
I+Sinatra
I+Shake
I+Freeze
I+Santiago de Cuba
I+Fire
I+Strawberry
I+YMCA
I+Lady Day
I+Tea
I+Salt+Pepper
I+Moloko
I+Love
I+Poison
I+Gin
I+Ice
I+Mint
I+Moscow

+Bordeaux
I+Sinatra
I+Shake
I+Freeze
I+Santiago de Cuba
I+Fire
I+Strawberry
I+YMCA
I+Lady Day
I+Tea
I+Salt+Pepper
I+Moloko
I+Love
I+Poison
I+Gin
I+Ice
I+Mint
I+Moscow

I+Drink On Tour

Tom Collins

- Gin
- Zumo de Limón
- Almíbar de Cereza
- Marraschino
- Rodaja de Limón
- Soda

Collin Teo
B OPTOM (UNSW)

39 Stamford Road
01-06 Stamford House
Singapore 178885

T: 65 6338 3240
F: 65 6338 5791

the.eyeplace@pacific.net.sg
www.eye-place.com

Operating Hours
Mon, Wed to Sat: 11:30am to 8pm
Sun: 11:30am to 6pm
Closed on Tues & Public Holidays

Gift Certificate Nº

Date of Issue

Voucher is redeemable at The Eye Place only. Redemption must be made in full. Multiple vouchers can be combined.
Voucher is valid for two years from date of issue. Only original vouchers accompanied by an official serial number
and signature will be accepted. The Eye Place reserves the right to reject any voucher deemed invalid.

050

Eye Place identity

CL: Eye Place
BN: Optical boutique
DE: &Larry

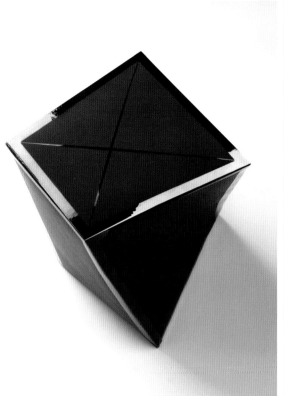

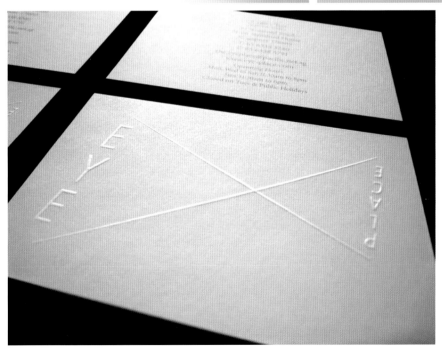

051

MIXTAPE GENERATION

CL: MIXTAPE GENERATION
BN: Design project
DE: Koji Sueyoshi

Carla

CL: Carla Grbac
BN: Textile designer, Weaver
DE: A Friend Of Mine
    Design Studio

CARLA GRBAC
WEAVER / ARTIST / JEWELER
WWW.CARLAGRBAC.COM
+61 (0)417 767 880

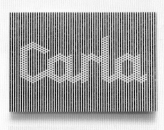

CARLA GRBAC IS A MAKER OF THINGS,
ENCHANTED BY THE IDEA OF MAKING CLOTH.
SHE COMBINES HER KNOWLEDGE OF ART,
WEAVING AND JEWELLERY TO CREATE
LIMITED EDITION WOVEN ORNAMENTS
AND ART PIECES TO ADORN THE BODY.

CALL OR EMAIL TO MAKE A STOCK INQUIRY
OR SEE EXAMPLES. BESPOKE PIECES ALSO
MADE TO ORDER.

WWW.CARLAGRBAC.COM
CARLAGRBAC@HOTMAIL.COM
+61 (0)438 376 880

Malota self-promotion

CL: Mar Hernéndez aka Malota
BN: Graphic designer,
Illustrator
DE: Malotaprojects

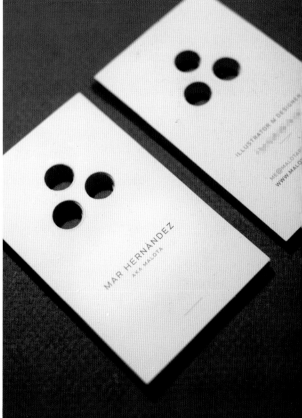

054
▬

Graphic Bar

CL: Graphic Bar
BN: Bar
DE: Umlaut

Futaba.

福田 大年
Hirotoshi Fukuda

fukuda@futabafutaba.org
090 7518 4940 M
011 211 1222 T/F

札幌市中央区北1条東2丁目5-4
ParkHills中央12-602
060 0031

Futaba.

児玉 美也子
Miyako Kodama
Designer / Illustrator

kodama@futabafutaba.org
090 6217 2462 M
011 211 1222 T/F

札幌市中央区北1条東2丁目5-4
ParkHills中央12-602
060 0031

055

Futaba.

CL: Futaba.
BN: Design firm
DE: Futaba.

TAKUTO KOSUKEGAWA

CL: Takuto Kosukegawa
BN: Photographer
DE: COMMUNE

KLJ

KLJ Solutions

CL: KLJ Solutions
BN: Specialist consultancy
DE: El Studio Limited

L'escalier identity

CL: L'escalier
BN: Art studio and retailer
DE: &Larry

391 ORCHARD ROAD
#04-20K NGEE ANN CITY
SINGAPORE 238872
T 6735 4228
E INFO@LESCALIER.COM.SG
WWW.LESCALIER.COM.SG

Kalideen

CL: Kalideen Acupuncture
BN: Acupuncturist
DE: Magpie Studio

kalideen
acupuncture

Shereen Kalideen
MA(hons), Dip Ac.
MBAcC

Contact
+44 (0)777 333 2864
shereen@kalideen.com
www.kalideen.com

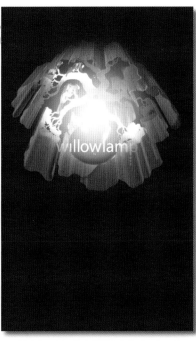

willowlamp.com

Sian Eliot
083 651 6772
info@willowlamp.com

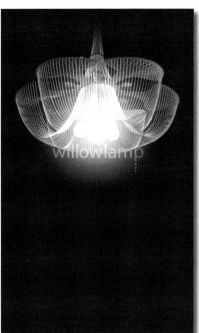

060

Willowlamp

CL: Willowlamp
BN: Product brand
DE: REX

061

925 Furniture

CL: 925 Furniture (Entry)
BN: Furniture company
DE: Justin Colt

062

Fifth Floor

CL: Fifth Floor
BN: Design firm and gallery
DE: Robert Apodaca

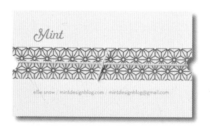

063

Mint

CL: Mint
BN: Blogger
DE: Hello Tenfold

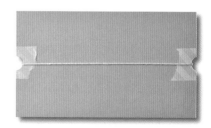

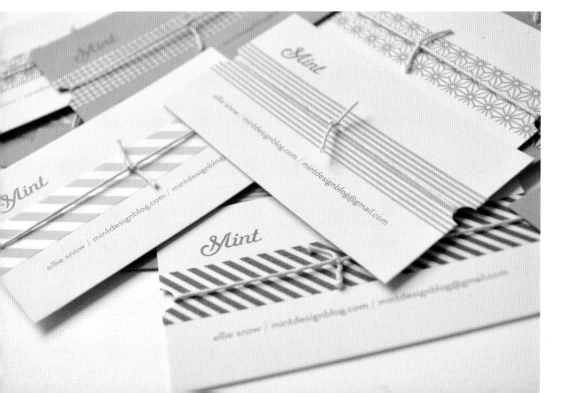

064
———

Paprika stationery

CL: Paprika.com
BN: Graphic design firm
DE: Paprika.com

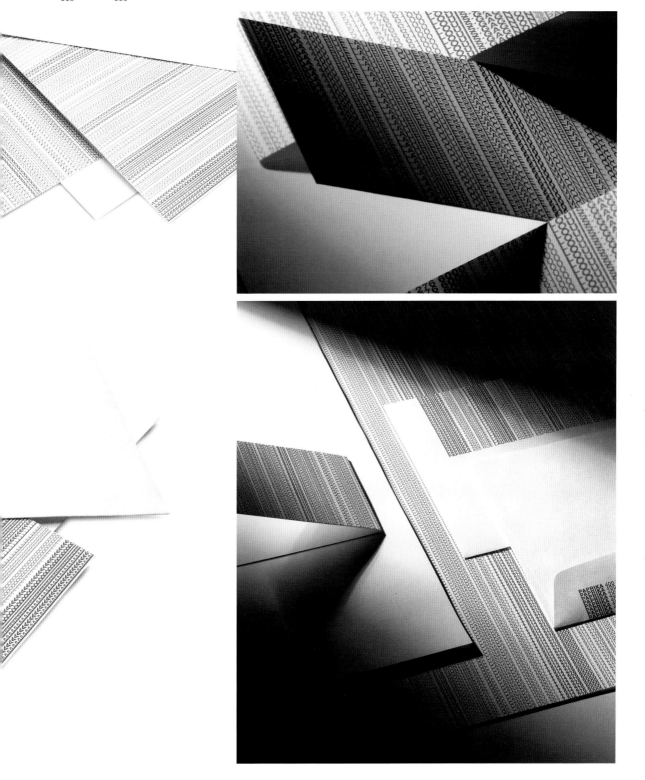

BEN —
DITA

GLO —
RIA

BEN — BEN —
DITA ITA

GLO GLO —
RIA

BEN —
DITA

GLO —
RIA

BEN — DITA

CL: Bendita Gloria
BN: Graphic design firm
DE: Bendita Gloria

066
———

Low Winter Sun branding

CL: Jonathan Atkinson
BN: Ethical consultancy
DE: Because Studio

LOW WINTER SUN

Jonathan Atkinson ——
jonathan@lowwintersun.info
0161 232 9292
0782 861 7933

OpenSpace Co-op
Unit 1, 41 Old Birley Street
Manchester M15 5RF

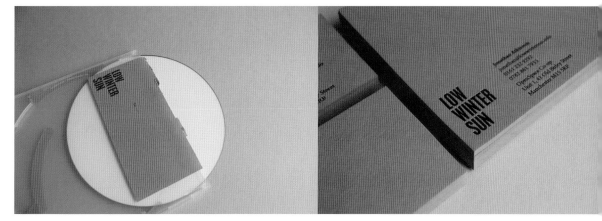

Blusyne restaurant identity

CL: Blusyne
BN: Restaurant
DE: DADADA studio

Margarita Ustinavičiūtė

+370 684 26 950
margo@ring.lt
www.blusyne.lt
Savičiaus g. 5

Darius Rutkys

+370 671 949 62
darius@ring.lt
www.blusyne.lt
Savičiaus g. 5

Vilnius, Savičiaus st. 5
+370 5 2125564
www.blusyne.lt

Vilnius, Savičiaus st. 5
+370 5 2125564
www.blusyne.lt

cafe place
Savičiaus st. 5

068

Burn Cottage

CL: Burn Cottage
BN: Biodynamic winery
DE: Mash

Thirdrow Films Visual Identity

CL: Thirdrow Films
BN: Film production company
DE: 21-19

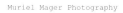

070

Muriel Mager Photography

CL: Muriel Mager
BN: Photographer
DE: almost Modern

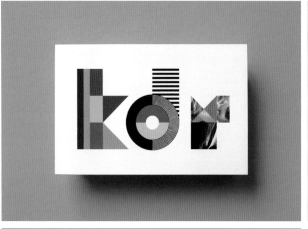
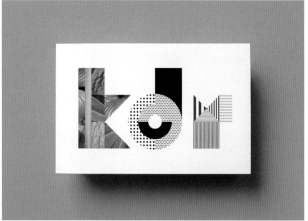
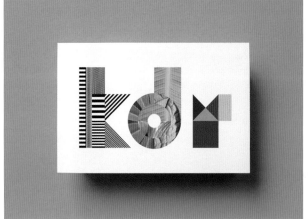
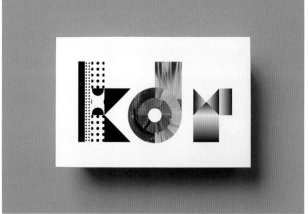

Naam Achternaam
+31 (0)6 123 456 78
naam@kdrprint.nl

Kwak & Van Daalen & Ronday Drukkerij B.V.
Kleine Tocht 13, 1507 CB Zaandam
telefoon +31 (0)75 631 04 01 – fax +31 (0)75 612 34 03
www.kdrprint.nl

Corporate identity for KDR (Proposal)

CL: Kwak & Van Daalen & Ronday (KDR)
BN: Printer
DE: CakeLab

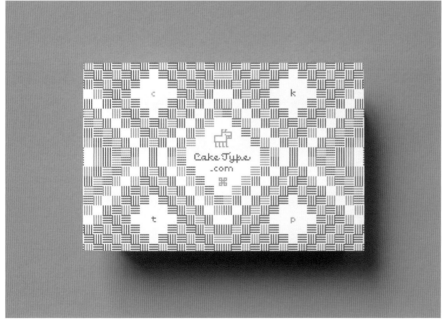

CakeType

CL: CakeType
BN: Digital type foundry
DE: CakeLab

073

K2

CL: Bron Durney
BN: Investment consultancy
DE: Wishart Design

Gabe Kemeny
Director

K2

K2 Investment Group Limited
PO Box 8701 Havelock North 4157
Farming House, Level 1
211 Market Street Sth
Hastings 4122 New Zealand
gkemeny@kemenys.com.au

telephone + 61 2 9380 7200
mobile + 61 4 1181 2081

Left Brain Right

CL: Yvonne Moxham
BN: Film producer
DE: Wishart Design

YVONNE MOXHAM

LEFT BRAIN RIGHT

+61 416 268 976
YVONNE@LEFTBRAINRIGHT.NET
WWW.LEFTBRAINRIGHT.NET

Toby Ng 伍廣圖
www.toby-ng.com
mail@toby-ng.com
UK +44 78 2591 2057
HK +852 6341 3611

075

My Business Card

CL: Toby Ng
BN: Graphic designer
DE: Toby Ng

ate

CL: ate
BN: Accountancy firm
DE: MusaWorkLab™

Airside company rebrand

CL: Airside
BN: Design agency
DE: Airside

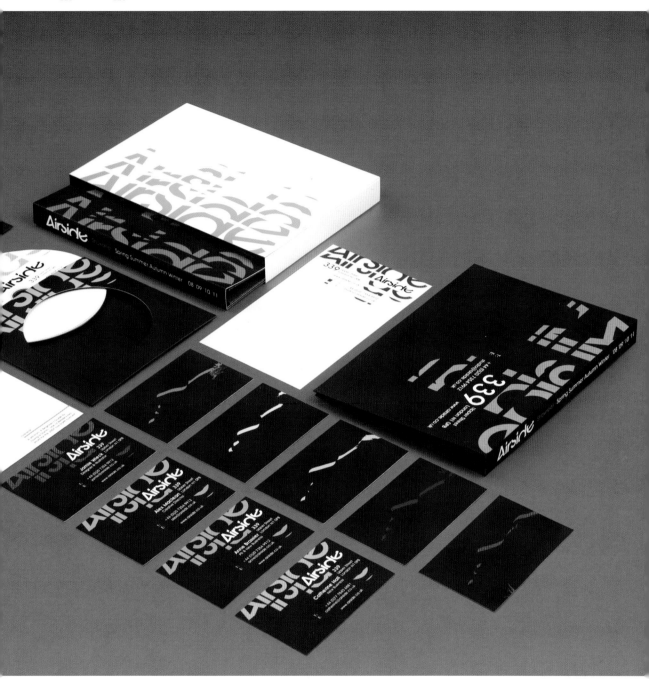

Pravina

CL: Pravina
BN: Fashion brand
DE: Vik LLC

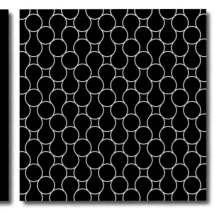

David Weik
Executive Creative Director
T 312 943 3333 **C** 312 543 7818
david@dentsulabs.com
dentsu Labs
213 West Institute Place, Unit 704
Chicago, Illinois 60622

Labs

CL: Labs
BN: Interactive design firm
DE: Vik LLC

Wooonderland identity

CL: Wooonderland
BN: Multi-brand boutique
DE: &Larry

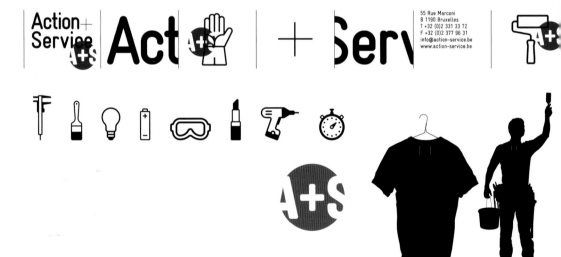

Action+Service identity

CL: Action+Service
BN: Production company
DE: Coast

Serv

Plan!
Create!
Build!
Check!
Trust!
Enjoy!
Share!

Day
Night

Action+

Plan!
Create!
Build!
Check!
Trust!
Enjoy!
Share!
Love!

Act

Action +
Service

{Lee Valentine}
Call +61 {2} 9302 9000
Suite 55, 61 Marlborough Street
Surry Hills NSW 2010 Australia

{email} info@29bikes.com.au
{website} www.29bikes.com.au

082

29 Bikes

CL: 29 Bikes
BN: Custom bicycle design firm
and retailer
DE: Tiana Vasiljev, Craig Johns

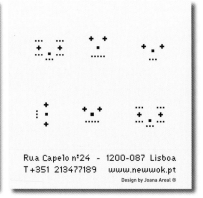

NEW WOK

CL: NEW WOK
BN: Noodle shop
DE: thisislove studio

Vegi Bar

CL: The Vegetable Bar
BN: Impromptu bar
DE: Magpie Studio

7pm—3am

Freiburg Markthalle
Kaiser-Joseph-Strasse
79098 Freiburg
00 49 (0) 761 7043 3155

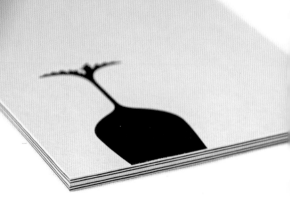

White wine
bottle/glass

25/7	Oveja Negra Chardonnay/Viognier Casablanca, Chile 2004
30/8	Domaines Felines-Jourdan Picpoul de Pinet Southern France 2004
30/8	Dr Loosen Blue Slate Riesling Mosel, Germany 2003
32	Knappstein Three Riesling Clare Valley, Australia 2004
40	D'Arenberg The Money Spider Roussanne McLaren Vale, Australia 2004
48	Alexia Sauvignon Blanc Nelson, New Zealand, 2004
53	Benefizium Porer Pinot Grigio Alois Lageder Alto Adige, Italy 2003
70	Catena Alta Chardonnay Mendoza Argentina 2002

The Vegetable Bar
White

The Vegetable Bar
Red

The Vegetable Bar
Fizz

The Vegetable Bar
Beer

The Vegetable Bar
Brandy

XTRA identity

CL: XTRA
BN: Furniture retailer
DE: &Larry

XTRA
OFFICE

XTRA
CONTRACT

XTRA
DESIGNS

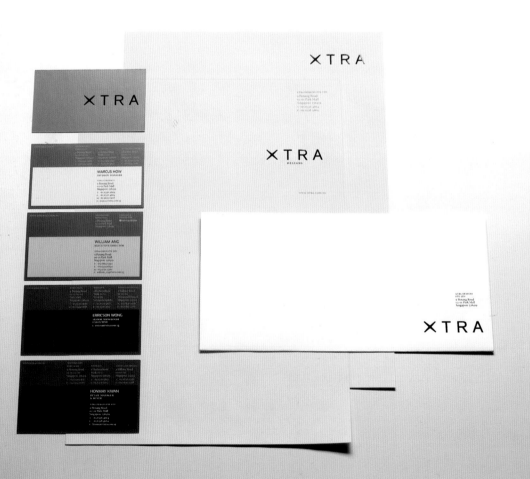

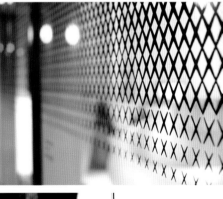

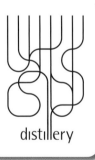

MATTHEW SHANG
CREATIVE DIRECTOR

DISTILLERY PTE LTD
4C ONE TREE HILL
SINGAPORE 248 672

T: 65.6732 6494 **M:** 65.9154 1050
E: MATTHEWSHANG@DISTILLERYSTUDIO.NET
W: WWW.DISTILLERYSTUDIO.NET

Distillery

CL: Distillery Pte Ltd
BN: Interior design consultancy
DE: SILNT

PAUL SEMPLE
DIRECTOR

DISTILLERY PTE LTD
4C ONE TREE HILL
SINGAPORE 248 672

T: 65.6732 6494 **M:** 65.9176 3720
E: PAULSEMPLE@DISTILLERYSTUDIO.NET
W: WWW.DISTILLERYSTUDIO.NET

MATTHEW SHANG
CREATIVE DIRECTOR

DISTILLERY PTE LTD
4C ONE TREE HILL
SINGAPORE 248 672

T: 65.6732 6494 **M:** 65.915
E: MATTHEWSHANG
W: WWW.DISTIL

Diane Gray-Smith identity

CL: Diane Gray-Smith
BN: Financial advisor
DE: Here Design

MANILA S.R.L.
VIA MONTE ZEBIO, 23
36030 CALDOGNO (VI)
T. +39 0444 903111
F. +39 0444 903150

info@maurogrifoni.com
www.maurogrifoni.com
P.I. 02570150249

MGNERD branding

CL: MGNERD by MAURO GRIFONI
BN: Fashion brand
DE: YOU

Big by Fiona Scanlan identity

CL: Big by Fiona Scanlan
BN: Fashion brand
DE: Studio Round

Limo_kids

CL: Limobebe
BN: Boutique
DE: emeyele®

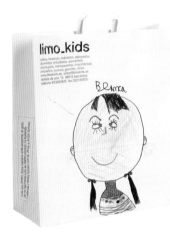

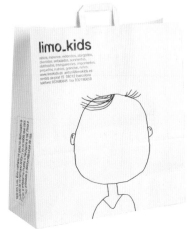

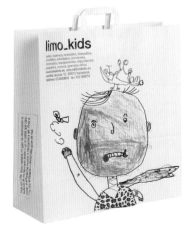

Eat Innovations identity

CL: Eat Innovations
BN: Marketing consultancy
DE: Ptarmak

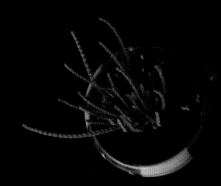

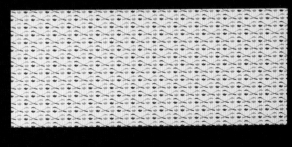

Massive

CL: Massive Productions
BN: Events agency
DE: Root

093

Insitu identity

CL: Insitu
BN: Commercial furniture supplier
DE: Qube Konstrukt

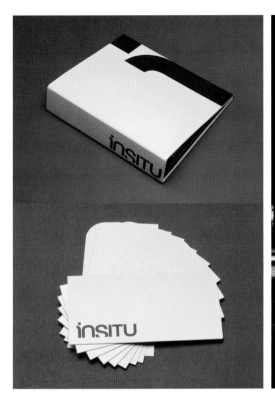

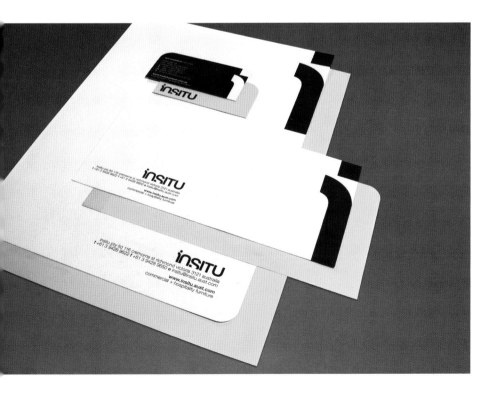

THE ONE THAT GOT

THE ONE THAT GOT AWAY (THE FISH SHOP)
FISHMONGER ONLINE (THE ONLINE DELIVERY)

AWAY

BARRY RALLIS (MANAGING DIRECTOR)

163 BONDI ROAD BONDI NSW 2026
TELEPHONE (02) 9389 4227 FACSIMILE (02) 9389 4227
MONDAY TO SUNDAY (8.00AM TO 9.00PM)

EMAIL BARRY@FISHMONGERONLINE.COM.AU
WEBSITE WWW.THEONETHATGOTAWAY.COM.AU

ONLINE

BARRY RALLIS (MANAGING DIRECTOR)

163 BONDI ROAD BONDI NSW 2026
TELEPHONE (02) 9389 4227 FACSIMILE (02) 9389 4227
MONDAY TO SUNDAY (8.00AM TO 9.00PM)

EMAIL BARRY@FISHMONGERONLINE.COM.AU
WEBSITE WWW.THEONETHATGOTAWAY.COM.AU

AWARDED

BARRY RALLIS (MANAGING DIRECTOR)

163 BONDI ROAD BONDI NSW 2026
TELEPHONE (02) 9389 4227 FACSIMILE (02) 9389 4227
MONDAY TO SUNDAY (8.00AM TO 9.00PM)

EMAIL BARRY@FISHMONGERONLINE.COM.AU
WEBSITE WWW.THEONETHATGOTAWAY.COM.AU

SOLD OUT

BARRY RALLIS (MANAGING DIRECTOR)

163 BONDI ROAD BONDI NSW 2026
TELEPHONE (02) 9389 4227 FACSIMILE (02) 9389 4227
MONDAY TO SUNDAY (8.00AM TO 9.00PM)

EMAIL BARRY@FISHMONGERONLINE.COM.AU
WEBSITE WWW.THEONETHATGOTAWAY.COM.AU

094
___

The One That Got Away

CL: The One That Got Away
BN: Fish and chips shop
DE: Tiana Vasiljev, Craig Johns

095

Rice 5 with Augmented Reality
technology

CL: Rice 5
BN: Interactive and digitial
advertising agency
DE: Rice 5

Huddle design

Dr Melis Senova
Director

M: 0400 749 585   6/443 Little Collins St
melis@huddledesign.com   Melbourne 3000

Huddle

CL: Huddle Design
BN: Strategic business consultancy
DE: A Friend Of Mine Design Studio

097

A Friend Of Mine

CL: A Friend Of Mine Design Studio
BN: Graphic design agency
DE: A Friend Of Mine Design Studio

SarkissianMason

Patrick Sarkissian
President

Mobile 917.443.4265 **Office** 212.625.8212
Fax 212.929.0791
patrick@sarkissianmason.com

135 W. 26th St., Floor 5, New York City, NY 10001
sarkissianmason.com

Michael Zaro
Executive Producer

Mobile 917.699.2049 **Office** 212.625.8212
Fax 212.929.0791
mz@sarkissianmason.com

135 W. 26th St., Floor 5, New York City, NY 10001
sarkissianmason.com

Matthew Schneider
Creative Director

Mobile 415.786.2769 **Office** 212.625.8212
Fax 212.929.0791
mmo@sarkissianmason.com

135 W. 26th St., Floor 5, New York City, NY 10001
sarkissianmason.com

Niki Shelley
Producer

Mobile 646.577.7957 **Office** 212.625.8212
Fax 212.929.0791
ns@sarkissianmason.com

135 W. 26th St., Floor 5, New York City, NY 10001
sarkissianmason.com

Zulema Arroyo
Partner/President Multicultural

Mobile 714.658.5549 **Office** 212.625.8212
Fax 212.929.0791
zulema@sarkissianmason.com

135 W. 26th St., Floor 5, New York City, NY 10001
sarkissianmason.com

098

Sarkissian Mason identity

CL: Sarkissian Mason
BN: Interactive design firm
DE: Carefully Considered, Hafez Janssens

Deco House

Etunimi Sukunimi

Oy Deco House Ab
Lemuntie 3–5, 00510 Helsinki, Finland
Tel +358 (0)00 000 0000 Fax +358 (0)00 000 0000
Direct +358 (0)00 000 0000 Mobile +358 (0)00 000 0000
etunimi.sukunimi@decohouse.fi

www.vallilainterior.fi

VALLILA

Vallila Interior

Etunimi Sukunimi

Tel +358 (0)00 0000 000 Fax +358 (0)00 0000 000
Direct +358 (0)00 0000 000 Mobile +358 (0)00 000 000
Email etunimi.sukunimi@vallilainterior.fi
Nilsiänkatu 15, 00150 Helsinki, Finland
www.vallilainterior.fi

Oy Vallila Interior Ab

Keha

Etunimi Sukunimi

Tel +358 (0)00 0000 000 Fax +358 (0)00 0000 000
Direct +358 (0)00 0000 000 Mobile +358 (0)00 000 000
Email etunimi.sukunimi@keha.fi
Nilsiänkatu 15, 00150 Helsinki, Finland
www.vallilainterior.fi

Oy Vallila Interior Ab

VIC

Etunimi Sukunimi

Tel +358 (0)00 0000 000 Fax +358 (0)00 0000 000
Direct +358 (0)00 0000 000 Mobile +358 (0)00 000 000
Email etunimi.sukunimi@vallilainterior.fi
Nilsiänkatu 15, 00150 Helsinki, Finland
www.vallilainterior.fi

Oy Vallila Interior Ab

Interia

Etunimi Sukunimi

Tel +358 (0)00 0000 000 Fax +358 (0)00 0000 000
Direct +358 (0)00 0000 000 Mobile +358 (0)00 000 000
Email etunimi.sukunimi@vallilainterior.fi
Nilsiänkatu 15, 00150 Helsinki, Finland
www.vallilainterior.fi

Oy Vallila Interior Ab

New identity for Vallila Interior

CL: Vallila Interior
BN: Interior and textile design collectives
DE: Kokoro & Moi

VALLILA
www.vallilainterior.fi
VALLILA
www.vallilainterior.fi
VALLILA
Deco House
VALLILA
Deco House
VALLILA
Deco House

VALLILA
Syksy
10
Hinnasto
VALLILA

Radar Festival

CL: Radar Festival
BN: Music festival
DE: Adam Morris

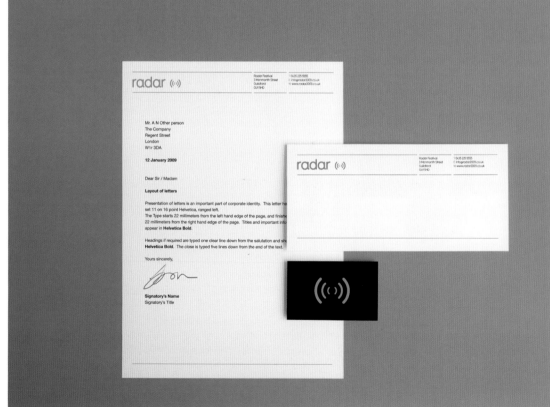

101

PataPri

CL: PataPri
BN: Textile designer
DE: Yuko Uemura

102
___

St George's Crypt

CL: St George's Crypt
BN: Christian charity
DE: B&W Studio

103
▬

STUDIOCO

CL: STUDIOCO
BN: Industrial design collective
DE: Studio Lin

EspaceFine

CL: EspaceFine
BN: Curator
DE: Pied de mouche

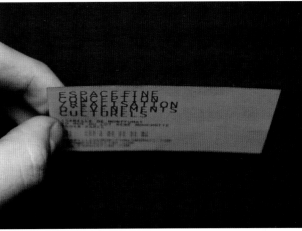

105

OIL

CL: OIL
BN: Research company
DE: REX

Studio 8a
32–60 Alice Street
Newtown NSW 2042 Australia
www.chrischen.com.au

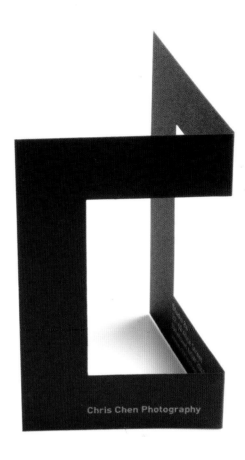

Chris Chen Photography

106
___

Chris Chen Photography identity

CL: Chris Chen Photography
BN: Photography studio
DE: Design By Pidgeon

Keith Fahy
M+353 (0)86 252 3862

Unit 16/17 Fashion City
Ballymount Road Upper
Dublin 24
Ireland

P+353 (0)1 429 3806
F+353 (0)1 429 3802
keith@wigwamevents.com
www.wigwamevents.com

107

Wigwam ID and branding

CL: Wigwam events
BN: Events management company
DE: Jamie Delaney

G-MAN

CL: G-MAN
BN: Graphic designer
DE: G-MAN

Loose Collective
••••••••••••••••••••••••••••••••••
Loose Collective
••••••••••••••••••••••••••••••••••
Graham Jones
+44 (0)773 275 2698
gman@loosecollective.net
••••••••••••••••••••••••••••••••••
www.loosecollective.net
••••••••••••••••••••••••••••••••••

Loose Collective

CL: Loose Collective
BN: Multi-disciplinary
creative collective
DE: G-MAN

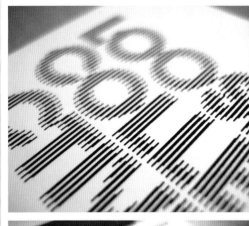

Loose Collective
•••••••••••••••••••••••••••••••••••••
Graham Jones
+44 (0)773 275 2698
gman@loosecollective.net
•••••••••••••••••••••••••••••••••••••
www.loosecollective.net
•••••••••••••••••••••••••••••••••••••

Loose Collective
•••••••••••••••••••••••••••••••
Gary Peploe
+44 (0)794 762 4208
gary@loosecollective.net
•••••••••••••••••••••••••••••••
www.loosecollective.net
•••••••••••••••••••••••••••••••

Som De Lisboa

CL: Som De Lisboa
BN: Sound production company
DE: MusaWorkLab™

111

The Creative Method

CL: The Creative Method
BN: Graphic design firm
DE: The Creative Method

ALGUIENVOLO identity

CL: ALGUIENVOLO
BN: Film production company
DE: LOSIENTO

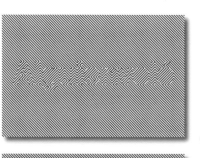

Alguienvoló
Audiovisual&Arts

Pau Claris 139 2º-1ª
Barcelona 08009
T +34 934676136
info@alguienvolo.com
www.alguienvolo.com

Esther Ruiz
Productora Ejecutiva

Alguienvoló
Audiovisual&Arts
Pau Claris 139 2º-1ª
Barcelona 08009
T +34 934676136
e.ruiz@alguienvolo.com
www.alguienvolo.com

Isis: Brand identity & stationery

CL: Isis Productions
BN: Film production agency
DE: Design Friendship

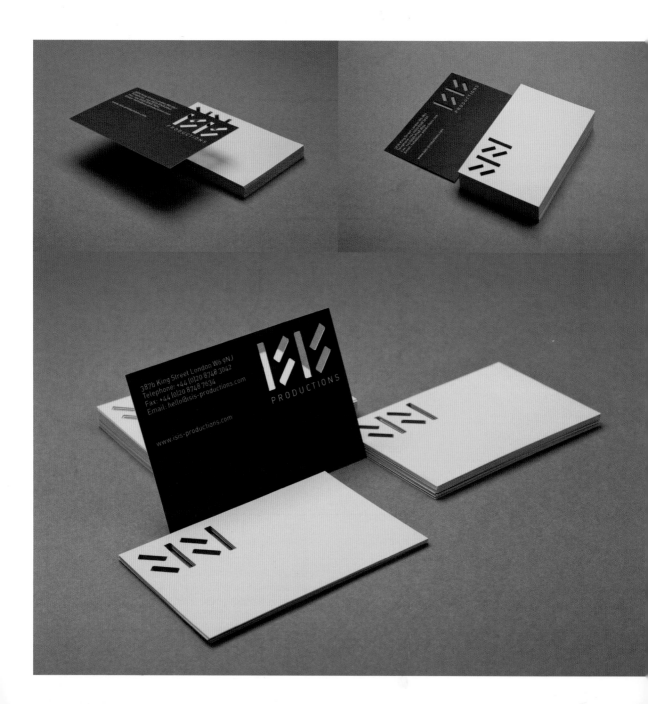

Barbershop identity

CL: Barbershop
BN: Music and sound design company
DE: Here Design

Identity Trapped in Suburbia

CL: Trapped in Suburbia
BN: Design and advertising agency
DE: Trapped in Suburbia

Marisa de Madariaga

Almagro 36 2ª pl.
28010 madrid
t.+34 91 310 72 60
f.+34 91 417 76 68
www.el-laboratorio.es
mdemadariaga@el-laboratorio.es

Carlos Holemans

Almagro 36 2ª pl.
28010 madrid
t.+34 91 310 72 60
f.+34 91 417 76 68
www.el-laboratorio.es
holemans@el-laboratorio.es

José Luis Gil

Almagro 36 2ª pl.
28010 madrid
t.+34 91 310 72 60
f.+34 91 417 76 68
www.el-laboratorio.es
jlgil@el-laboratorio.es

Mar Frutos

Almagro 36 2ª pl.
28010 madrid
t.+34 91 310 72 60
f.+34 91 417 76 68
www.el-laboratorio.es
marfrutos@el-laboratorio.es

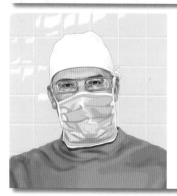

Antonio Pacheco

Almagro 36 2ª pl.
28010 madrid
t.+34 91 310 72 60
f.+34 91 417 76 68
www.el-laboratorio.es
pach@el-laboratorio.es

Rafael Silvela

Almagro 36 2ª pl.
28010 madrid
t.+34 91 310 72 60
f.+34 91 417 76 68
www.el-laboratorio.es
rsilvela@el-laboratorio.es

Manuel Montes

Almagro 36 2ª pl.
28010 madrid
t.+34 91 310 72 60
f.+34 91 417 76 68
www.el-laboratorio.es
manuelmontes@el-laboratorio.es

Laboratorio

CL: Laboratorio
BN: Publicity agency
DE: mirinda company
IL: Marta Zafra

el laboratorio

el laboratorio

el laboratorio

el laboratorio

el laboratorio

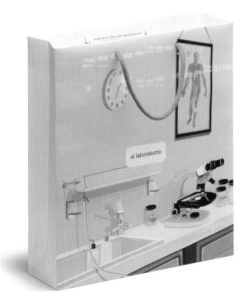

el laboratorio

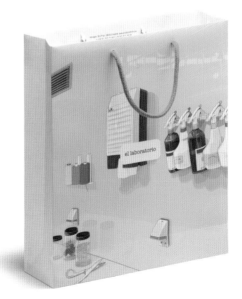

el laboratorio

REX Company Compendium

CL: REX
BN: Brand consultancy
DE: REX

REX CREATIVE WE ARE NOT DEFINED BY THE MEDIUM WE
WORK IN. WE ARE DEFINED BY OUR ABILITY TO SOLVE
PROBLEMS, BEAUTIFULLY. BLOCK E HURLINGHAM OFFICE
PARK WOODLANDS ROAD HURLINGHAM 2196 JHB PO
BOX 41612 CRAIGHALL 2024 JHB TEL 0117815442 FAX
0113261964 RECEPTION@REX.JHB.COM REX.JHB.COM

Design is go
Design is possi
successfully inte
to create compell
rex.jhb.com

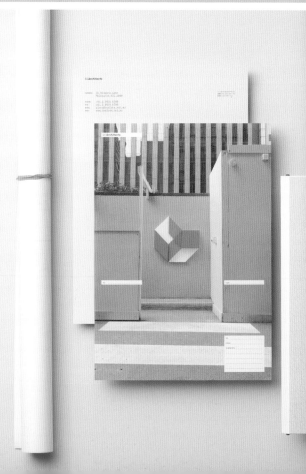

118

1.1 Architects

CL: 1.1 Architects
BN: Architecture firm
DE: Coöp

ELYA

CL: ELYA
BN: Sound production company
DE: LOSIENTO

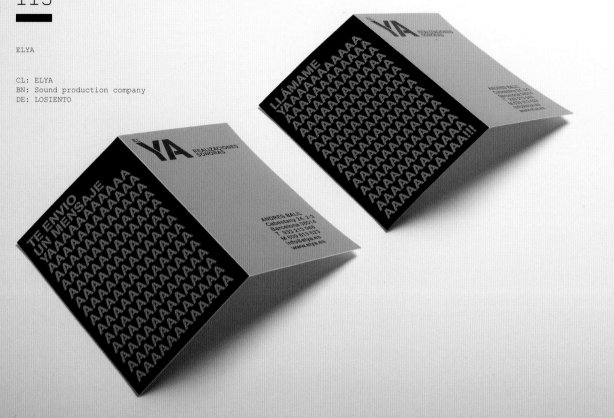

5ºPINO

CL: 5ºPINO
BN: Restaurant
    and bar
DE: LOSIENTO

MACHELL BUILDING CONTRACTORS
12 ST JOHN'S ROAD, YEADON
LEEDS LS19 7ND WEST YORKSHIRE
TELEPHONE: 0113 2505287
MOBILE: 07979 300 837

GLEN MACHELL
BRICKLAYER

121

Machells Building Contractors

CL: Machells Building Contractors
BN: Building contractor
DE: B&W Studio

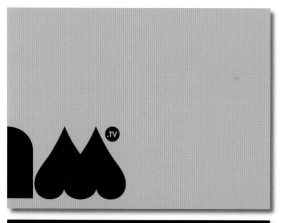

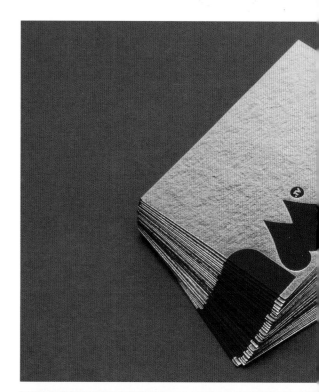

CREAM.TV   WWW.CREAMFILM.TV

RENAISSANCE HOUSE
28 OAKVILLE ROAD
WILLOUGHBY SYDNEY 2068

T/ +612 9967 0000
F/ +612 9967 8666
E/ CREAM@CREAMFILM.TV

Cream identity

CL: Cream Films
BN: Film production company
DE: Qube Konstrukt

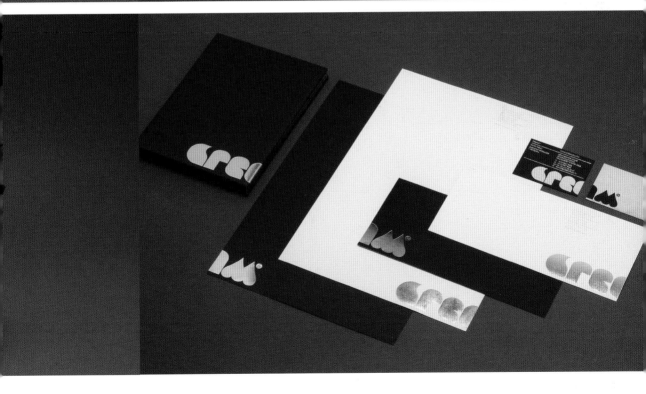

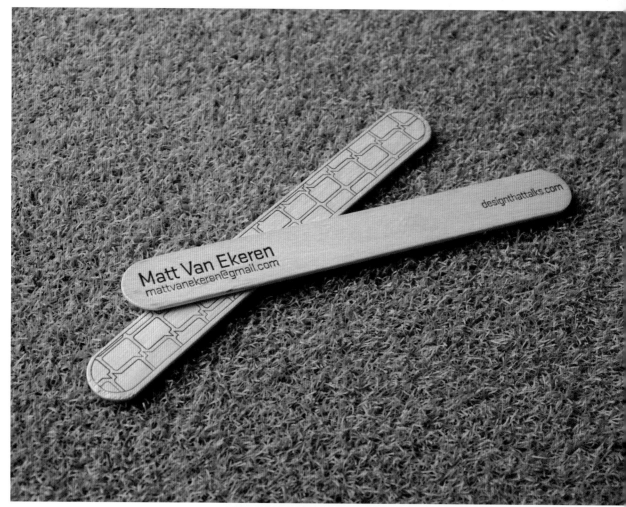

Tongue Depressor

CL: Design that talks
BN: Graphic Design firm
DE: Matt Van Ekeren

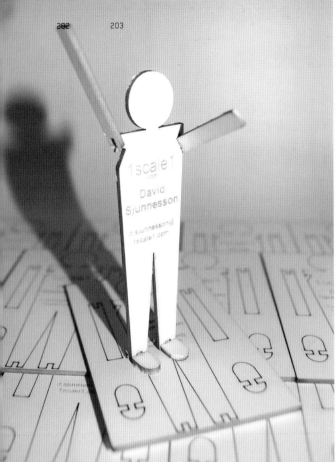

1scale1

CL: 1scale1
BN: Interactive design firm
DE: 1scale1

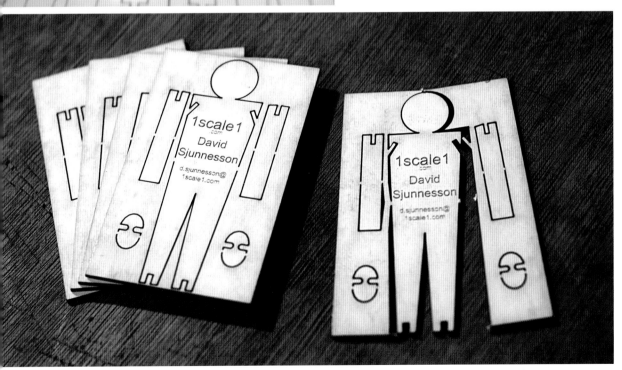

Pipsqueek IN SAIGON

t 08 8363 9577
f 08 8363 9677

appointment time

belinda
hair fairy

date

m 0405 508 697

Shop 1, No.1 Payneham Rd, College Park SA 5069
www.pipsqeekinsaigon.com

Pipsqueek IN SAIGON

t 08 8363 9577
f 08 8363 9677

aleisha
clothing karma

m 0405 347 344

Shop 1, No.1 Payneham Rd, College Park SA 5069
www.pipsqeekinsaigon.com

Pipsqueek in Saigon

Pipsqueek in Saigon, an exodus of genetic freedom, as salon spaces and retail disciplines are melded

... the 8th of October, you are cordially invit to take a jumpstart screening of their wor
ay 6th
at Shop
m Rd,
be early.

ovided)

Pipsqueek In Saigon

CL: Pipsqueek In Saigon
BN: Boutique
DE: Mash

Topaz Leung

CL: Topaz Leung
BN: Photographer, Writer, Stylist
DE: Disinlok, Topaz Leung

Smiley

CL: Driv Loo
BN: Graphic designer
DE: Driv Loo

EXPOSITION
des Diplômes Supérieurs des Arts Appliqués **2006/2007**
Olivier de Serres

Le jeudi 28 juin 2007 de 9h à 17h à la Mairie du XV° - Salle des fêtes

**École Nationale Supérieure
des Arts Appliqués et Métiers d'Arts**
Olivier de Serres

Avec le concours de la Mairie du XV°
Avec le concours du Fonds Social Européen

**École Nationale
Supérieure
des Arts Appliqués
et Métiers d'Arts**
Olivier de Serres
www.ensaama.net

128

DSAA EXPO

CL: ENSAAMA Olivier de Serres .
BN: Art and design school
DE: Frédéric Tacer and Yorel Cayla

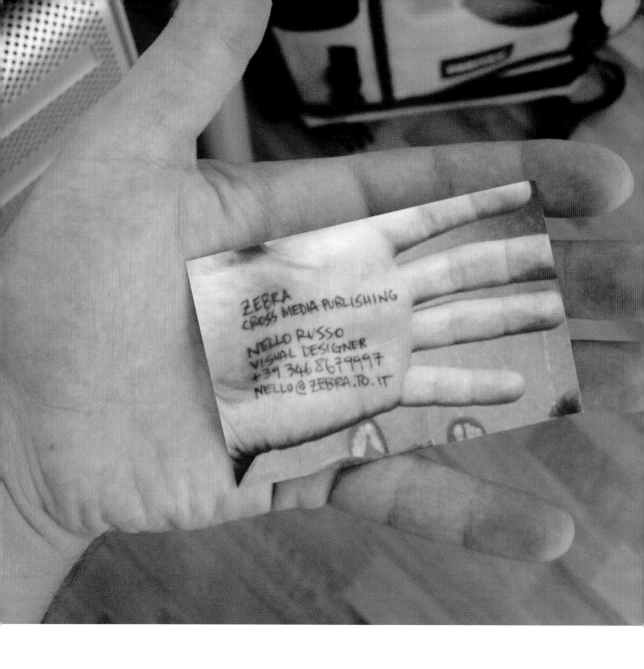

129

ZEBRA

CL: ZEBRA Graphic design agency
BN: Graphic design agency
DE: Nello Russo

ZEBRA è un'agenzia creativa con sede a Torino in via Verdi 12, 10124.
Tel. e fax +39 011 8136068 www.zebra.to.it

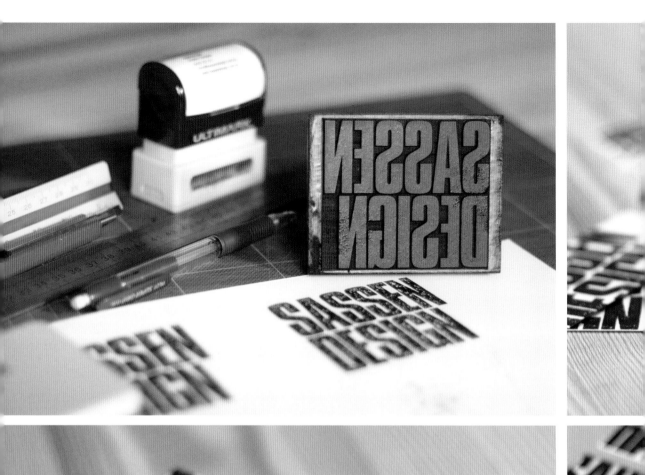

130

Sassen Design

CL: Sassen Design
BN: Design firm
DE: Sassen Design

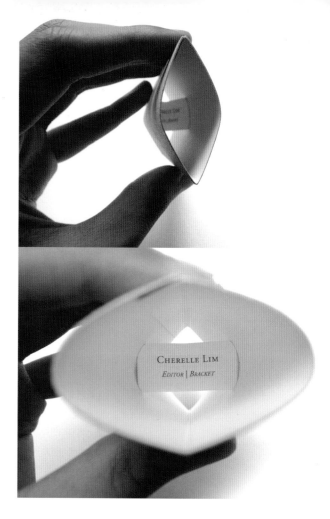

131

Bracket

CL: Bracket
BN: Publication
DE: SILNT

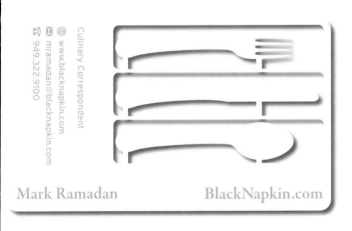

132

CL: Black Napkin
BN: Blogger
DE: Mark Ramadan

SO-AND-SO

CL: SO-AND-SO
BN: Publishing firm
DE: Nello Russo

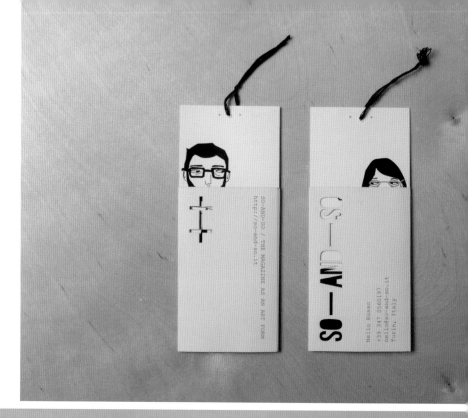

Another Bloomin' Designer

CL: Jamie Wieck
BN: Graphic designer, Illustrator
DE: Jamie Wieck

Measurements: 12 pt = 1 pica / 1 pica = 0.1667 in / 2p4 means 2 picas and 4 points / 6 pica = 1 in

Ideal line length: about 66 characters.

Dashes: set off phrases—em dash with no spaces—en dashes denote up to and including (1918-1945).

Ellipsis: … [full space . thin space . thin space . full space] ⣿

Also: "quote 'within' quote" / small caps can be used for acronyms: NATO, ROFL / times: 3:27AM

Other little things: 5′8″ (use primes) / St, Dr, Ms, Ave, etc (no period) / 2,021 / 2 × 3.5 in / 4 cm / *eg* this / *ie* that / p.163-170 / c.1940 / *Things fall apart* by W B Yeats

1 References: *The elements of typographic style* by Robert Bringhurst, *Type & typography* by Baines & Haslam, and a few bits of personal preference. ☺

Hello!

I am a lot of things; a writer, a cartographer, a typographer, (hopefully) human, a space traveler, a searcher, etc. I have an interest in film, history, urban planning, literature (and more!)

(I don't really like the idea of using all this paper (500 cards = 24 sq ft of paper) for only contact information. I decided to put a typography 'cheat sheet' on the back, I hope you may find it useful. Typeset in 7 pt Feijoa.)

Abi Huynh, B DES
typography & design
abi@mysterywesterntheory.com
www.mysterywesterntheory.com
www.abiabiabi.com

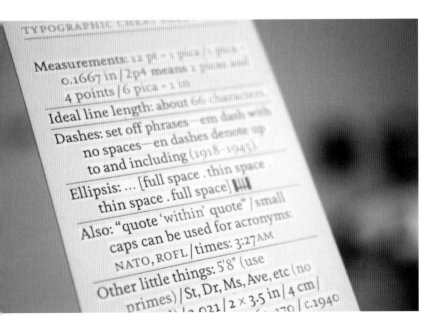

Abi Huynh

CL: Abi Huynh
BN: Graphic designer
DE: Abi Huynh

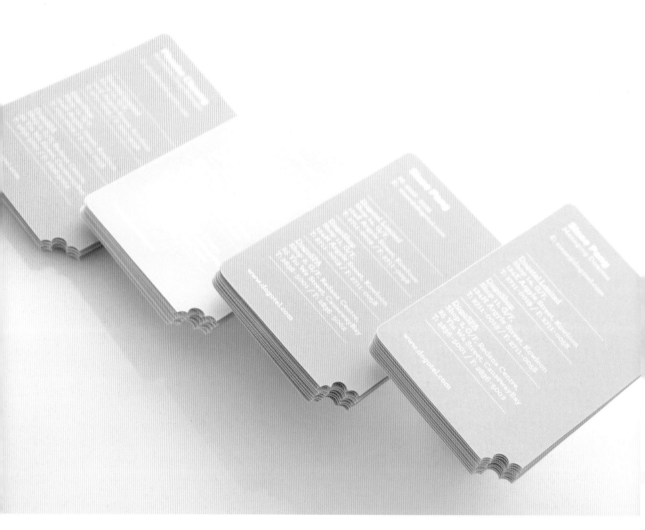

136

Dogotel

CL: Dogotel
BN: Pet service provider
DE: Studiowill

137

Visual identity Dutchtub

CL: Dutchtub
BN: Product brand
DE: Since 1416, graphic design & visual research

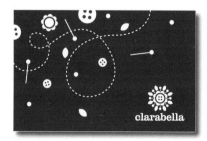

138
─────

Clarabella

CL: Clarabella
BN: Textile artist
DE: Studio MIKMIK

Claire Wellesley-Smith
Textile Artist & Workshop Leader
email claire@clarabella.co.uk phone 07912 241030 www.clarabella.co.uk

Pretty Green: Brand identity & stationery

CL: Pretty Green
BN: PR agency
DE: Design Friendship

140
___

OZ hair studio

CL: OZ hair studio
BN: Hair salon
DE: Recircle

Yuka Suzuki

CL: Yuka Suzuki
BN: Hairstylist,
    Makeup artist
DE: Studio Kudos

Stamp it CI

CL: Pixelgarten
BN: Design firm
DE: Pixelgarten

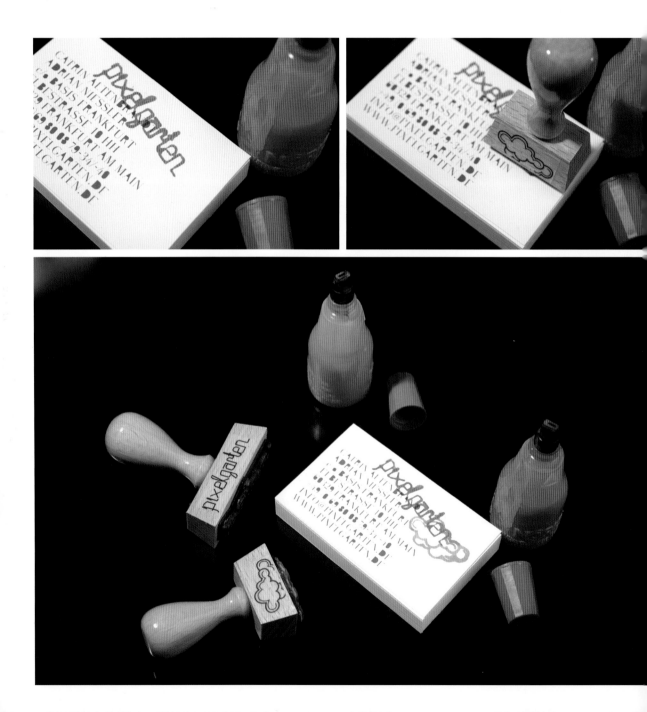

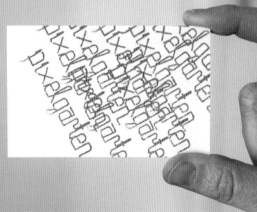

143
___

Playful

CL: Playful
BN: Graphic design firm
DE: Playful

playful

Pablo Alfieri
Graphic Design

(5411) 15 5481 3857
pablo@pabloalfieri.com
www.pabloalfieri.com

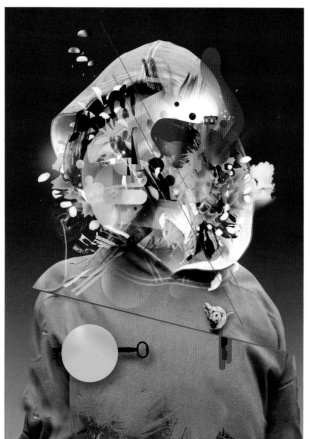

Mr & Mrs Ho

CL: Calvin Ho / Atomic Attack
BN: Design firm
DE: Calvin Ho / Atomic Attack

OCU

CL: OCU
BN: Insurance brokerage
DE: m Barcelona

OCU

Organització Caballé Urrutia . Corredoria d'Assegurances S.L.
Sicília 115 baixos . Barcelona 08013

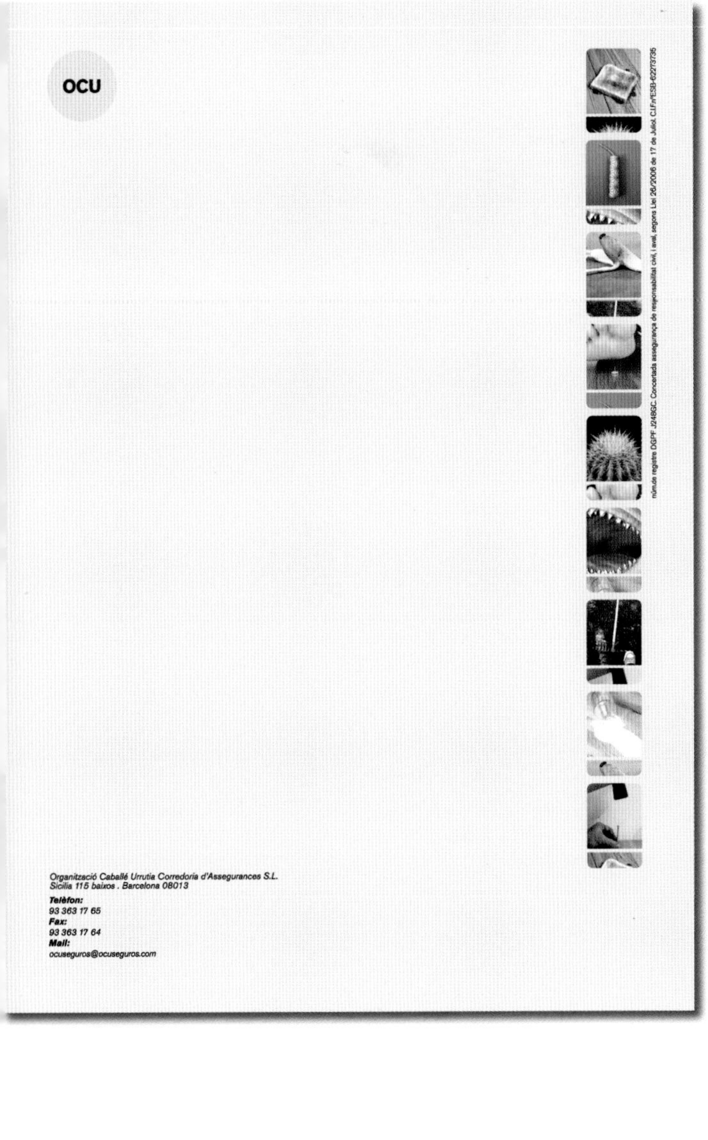

OCU

núm.de registre DGFP J2489GC. Concertada assegurança de responsabilitat civil, i aval, segons Llei 26/2006 de 17 de Juliol. CIF/r'ESB-62073735

OCU

Corredoria d'Assegurances S.L.
Sicília 115 baixos . Barcelona 08013

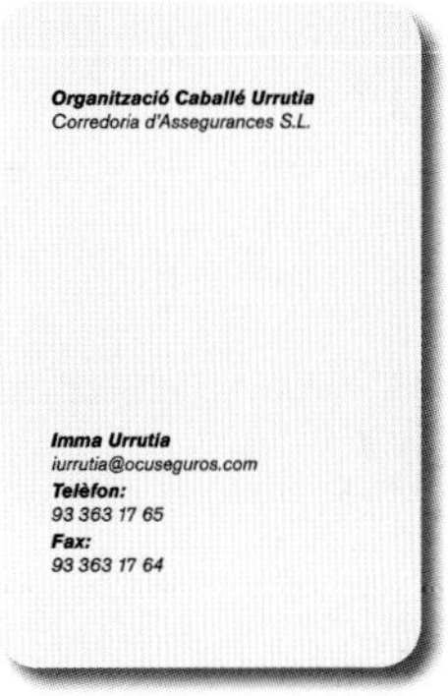

Organització Caballé Urrutia
Corredoria d'Assegurances S.L.

Imma Urrutia
iurrutia@ocuseguros.com
Telèfon:
93 363 17 65
Fax:
93 363 17 64

Organització Caballé Urrutia Corredoria d'Assegurances S.L.
Sicília 115 baixos . Barcelona 08013
Telèfon:
93 363 17 65
Fax:
93 363 17 64
Mail:
ocuseguros@ocuseguros.com

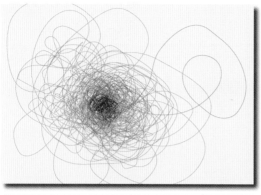

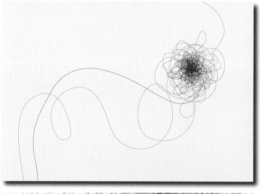

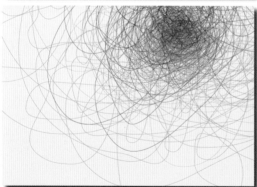

Jorge Virgós

CL: Jorge Virgós
BN: Brand consultancy
DE: m Barcelona

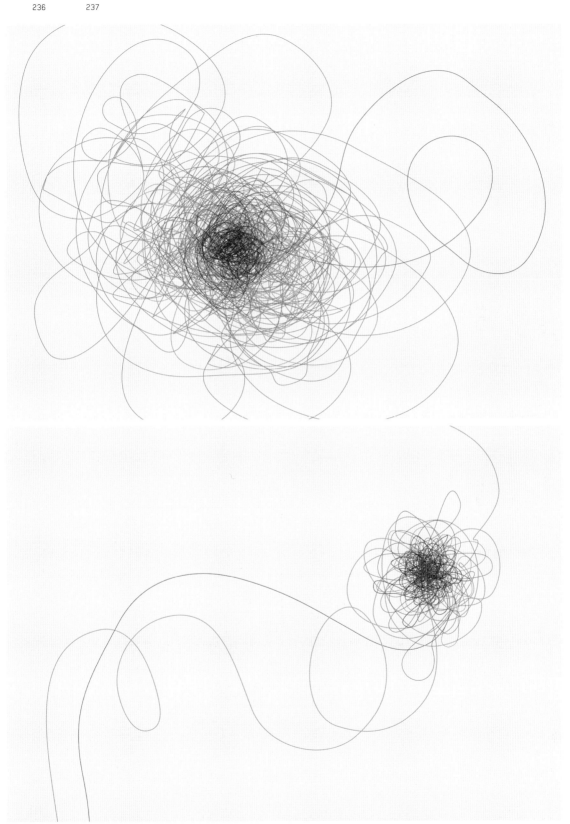

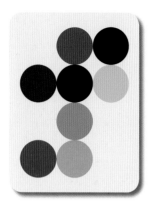

Pablo Álvarez Silva
Co-fundador / Presidente
pok: Pablo
e-mail: pablo@poksmedia.com
M: +34 636 068 539
T: +34 93 318 96 86

POKs Media, SL
Passeig de Gràcia, 11, Esc.A, 7º 2ª
08007 Barcelona, España

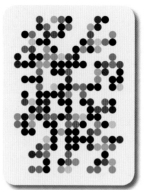

Sancho Pardo de Santayana
Co-fundador / Director General
pok: Sanchopst
e-mail: sancho@poksmedia.com
M: +34 690 822 803
T: +34 93 318 96 86

POKs Media, SL
Passeig de Gràcia, 11, Esc.A, 7º 2ª
08007 Barcelona, España

POK

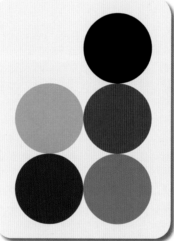

POK

Jordi Barri Carles
Marketing Manager

pok: Jordi
e-mail: jordi.barri@poksmedia.com
M: +34 609 88 28 66
T: +34 93 318 96 86

POKs Media, SL
Passeig de Gràcia, 11, Esc.A, 7º 2ª
08007 Barcelona, España

POK

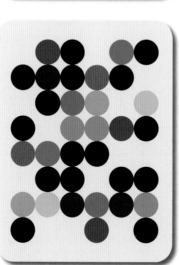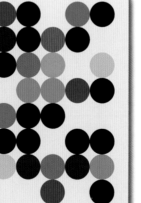

POK

Joan Casaponsa Sitjàs
Consejero delegado

pok: Joan
e-mail: jcasaponsa@poksmedia.com
M: +34 686 983 113
T: +34 93 318 96 86

POKs Media, SL
Passeig de Gràcia, 11, Esc.A, 7º 2ª
08007 Barcelona, España

CL: POK
BN: Mobile social networking service
DE: m Barcelona

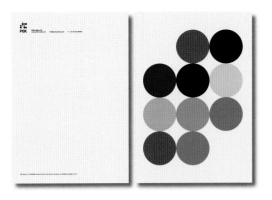

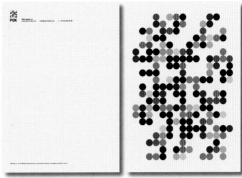

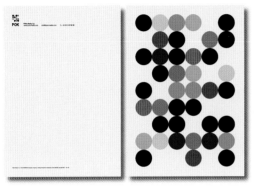

OK Great identity

CL: OK Great
BN: Multi-displinary
design collective
DE: OK Great

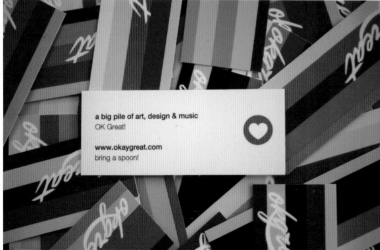

a big pile of art, design & music
OK Great!

www.okaygreat.com
bring a spoon!

Hanneke Beukers identity

CL: Hanneke Beukers project
& event management
BN: Project and event management firm
DE: saf~

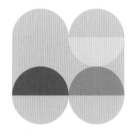

hannekebeukers.nl

hanneke beukers
project & event management
studio: staalkade 6 sous / 1011 jn amsterdam
info@hannekebeukers.nl / 0031 6 4778 2200

hanneke beukers
project & event management
studio: staalkade 6 sous / 1011 jn amsterdam
info@hannekebeukers.nl / 0031 6 4778 2200

hannekebeukers.nl

150

The Chop Shop identity & paper system

CL: The Chop Shop (self-initated project)
BN: Butcher shop and delicatessen
DE: Ptarmak

Penelope Christodoulidi

CL: Penelope Christodoulidi
BN: Photographer
DE: Kanella

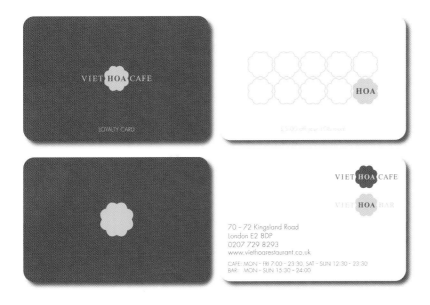

Viet Hoa Café & Bar

CL: Viet Hoa Café & Bar
BN: Restaurant and bar
DE: VONSUNG

Good co.

CL: Good Company
BN: Coffee Shop
DE: Landor Associates

Perky Bros identity

CL: Perky Bros LLC
BN: Graphic design firm
DE: Perky Bros LLC

Jefferson Perky   ART DIRECTOR / OWNER

1200 Clinton St Nº 221 Nashville TN 37203   ADDRESS

(615) / 760 5568 jeff@perkybros.com   PHONE / EMAIL

Morton & Peplow

CL: Morton & Peplow
BN: Fine dining restaurant
DE: Magpie Studio

10NT identity

CL: 10NT Collaborative
BN: Design collective
DE: Carefully Considered, Hafez
Janssens, IAAH / iamalwayshungry

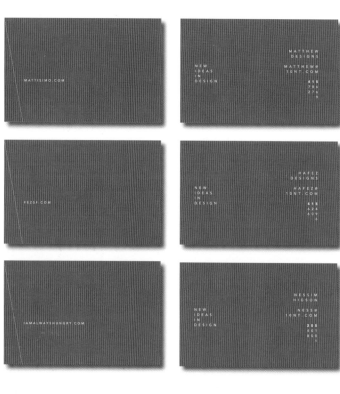

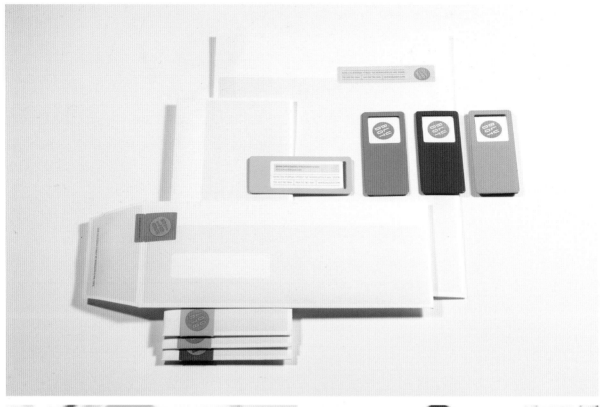

157

Bludot stationery

CL: Bludot Design & Manufacturing
BN: Furniture company
DE: Steven Jockisch

158

JAM

CL: Julie Adamson Miller
BN: Community arts operator
DE: Ryan Crouchman

CHICKEN PECKER

CL: CHICKEN PECKER
BN: Restaurant
DE: COMMUNE

Name Surname

Hive London
55 Warwick Way   Telephone: 020 7934 3422
London SW1V 1CR   Email: name@hivelondon.co.uk
United Kingdom   www.hivelondon.co.uk

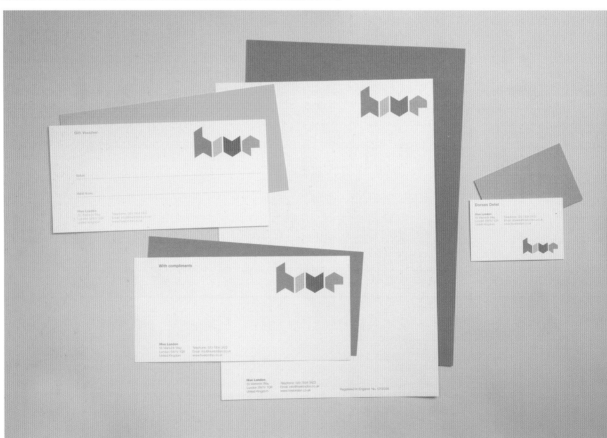

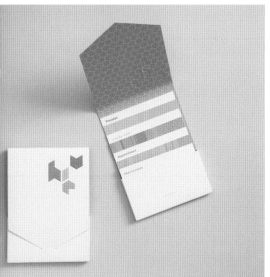

160

Hive

CL: Hive London
BN: Hair and beauty salon chain
DE: Mind Design, Emulsion Architecture

gumbo

Name Surname
+44 (0)1234 567 890
name@gumbo.tv

www.gumbo.tv

gUMbo

Name Surname
+44 (0)1234 567 890
name@gumbo.tv

www.gumbo.tv

Gumbo

Name Surname
+44 (0)1234 567 890
name@gumbo.tv

www.gumbo.tv

gumBo

Name Surname
+44 (0)1234 567 890
name@gumbo.tv

www.gumbo.tv

Gumbo

Name Surname
+44 (0)1234 567 890
name@gumbo.tv

www.gumbo.tv

Gumbo TV

CL: Paul Pethick
BN: Animation artist
DE: Mind Design

Paul Pethick
+44 (0)7768 362 575
pp@gumbo.tv
www.gumbo.tv

Name Surname

Tea Limited
12 Street Name
London AB12 3CD

Phone +44 (0)20 7123 4567
Fax +44 (0)20 7123 4567
Mobile +44 (0)1234 567 890
Email name@wearetea.com

www.wearetea.com

Tea

CL: Tea Limited
BN: Tea shop
DE: Mind Design

163

Aviary

CL: Aviary Fashion Boutique
BN: Boutique
DE: 21-19

To

For the value of

From

Valid to

Our #

High Street
Victoria 3442
fax 03 5427 2504
@freeasabird.com.au

aviary

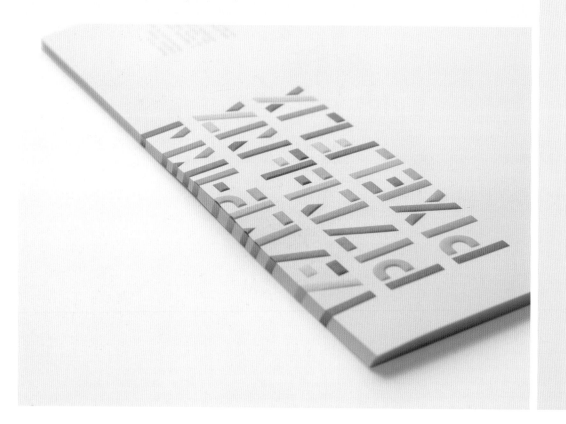

Pixelflix

CL: Pixelflix
BN: Digital production and
editing company
DE: A Friend Of Mine
Design Studio

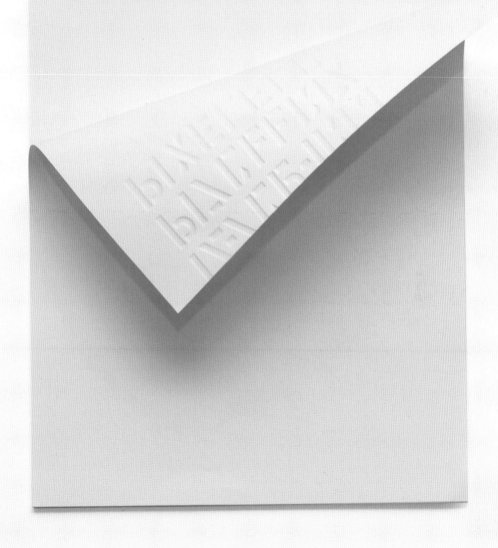

Pixel Flix
Digital Video
Production & Editing

5 Neptune Lane
St Kilda 3182
Vic, Australia
+61(0)405 092 203

www.pixelflix.com.au
ABN 94 233 879 021

Name Surname
Director

TESS Management
4TH Floor, 9–10 Market Place
London W1W 8AQ

T +44 (0)20 7557 7100
F +44 (0)20 7557 7101
M +44 (0)7899 688808
name@tessmanagement.com
www.tessmanagement.com

165

Tess Management

CL: Tess Management
BN: Model agency
DE: Mind Design, Simon Egli (Zurich)

TESS Management

info@tessmanagement.com • www.tessmanagement.com

001

SPECIFICATIONS

⤢ 75 x 85 mm

▱ Double Sided B & W
Mountboard 1200 Micron

✎ CMYK, Metallic Silver,
Metallic Gold

✳ Screenprint

Double-sided, with each of the unique trian-
gles hand-cut into shape, six variations of
eyes are screenprinted onto the thick, black
mount board in silver or gold to represent
Jordan Metcalf. Metcalf is a graphic designer and artist based in Cape Town, and he has
a love for typography, illustration, good
design, and the combination of the three.

002

SPECIFICATIONS

⤢ 88.9 x 50.8 mm

▱ GF Smith Pristine White
Colourplan Uncoated 175gsm
(Inside), Dark Grey
Colourplan Uncoated
350gsm (Outside)

✎ CMYK

✳ Die-cut

Jessica Walsh's business card is a miniature
portfolio itself, which contains five cards
in a card pocket, printed with Walsh's sam-
ples of work. While each of the works is accompanied with a brief project description,
year of work created and respective client's
name on the back, Walsh's initials die cut
on the pocket gives you a window to catch a
glimpse on her projects without a hitch.

003

SPECIFICATIONS

⤢ 55 x 85 mm

▱ 3 versions: Keaykolour
Sombre Grey, Savana Bub-
inga, Curious Skin Dark
Blue (300gsm Card) Sticotac
Offset 73gsm (Label)

✎ 4 PMS, 2 per card

✳ Sticker

MUR is an Portuguese architecture and interior design studio. Their business cards was
designed to build in visual narratives of
architectural projects and labels normally
seen on project panel boards were used, composing a smart and eye-catching identity on
the distinctively dark stock.

004

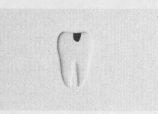

SPECIFICATIONS

⤢ 54 x 85 mm

▱ Cromulux

✎ CMYK, Fluorescent
Magenta & Violet

✳ -

This card doesn't need an explanation - you
will know what to do when you got tooth
decay.

005

SPECIFICATIONS

⤢ 50 x 90 mm

▱ Papierunion Senator
Smooth 308gsm

✎ CMYK, PMS 806 M

✳ Lamination

jungeschachtel has created themselves a
unique card to ressemble the experience
of 'opening up' the 'hidden' as when you
unpack a product. All in all, the card was
to tell the studio's major field of design
in packaging.

006

SPECIFICATIONS

⤢ 55 x 85 mm

▱ Munken Polar 400gsm

✎ CMYK, PMS 231, 871

✳ -

Opening its doors at Geneva International
Airport in 2008, Montreux Jazz Café offers
its clients a chance to immerse in the
mellow atmosphere of the half-century old
Montreux Jazz Festival in Switzerland.
Reminiscent of the classic backstage light
bulbs and the 'backstage' where archives of
the festival are shown, a dotted typeface
came out. The identity project encompasses
the café's menu, invitation, sugar packs
and packaging.

007

SPECIFICATIONS

- ⬈ 55 x 85 mm
- ▭ Spicers Paper Stephen Uncoated 330gsm
- ✎ CMYK
- ✳ Digital print

Kaffe is done for a coffee shop started by four Swedes, thus the name 'Kaffe', Swedish for 'coffee'. The very personal connection which every person has with Kaffe's coffee inspired the chalk handwriting. The work was intended to address their customers in a direct style of communication, via business cards, bags, takeaway cups etc.

008

SPECIFICATIONS

- ⬈ 55 x 90 mm
- ▭ Knight Linen 280gsm
- ✎ CMYK
- ✳ -

Kind of a contrast with the usual yellow cheesy impression, the goal of this project was to create a personal and unique solution for boutique cheese company, Over The Moon. Designed with the English nursery rhyme 'Hey diddle diddle' handwritten in a casual manner, the stationery and cheese wrappings are filled with a motherly nature in the cheese-making. The huge name on the business card says a friendly 'hi' to whoever holds the card.

009

SPECIFICATIONS

- ⬈ 50 x 85 mm, 65 x 85 mm (Card book)
- ▭ Opale Premier Pure White 300gsm
- ✎ PMS 877 U
- ✳ Lamination, Scratch ink

GSA Design's business card is like a scratch n' win game card – whoever scratches the ink wins... a contact! By covering personal contacts with a layer of scratch ink, the card functions as a personal and general card at the same time, with individual and general contacts to offer in different situations. GSA Design is a collective of designers who develop projects in graphic design and illustration at Porto, Portugal.

010

SPECIFICATIONS

- ⬈ 52 x 85 mm
- ▭ Scandia 2000 White 300gsm
- ✎ PMS 3005 U, 3405 U
- ✳ Emboss

First emerged in 2006, the identity for Swedish graphic designer Jens Nilsson's personal brand, dancemade, features a customised wood block typeface popular around many blogs by the time. The fonts are later blind-embossed on white card stock and produced as framed posters as a kind of decorative art.

011

SPECIFICATIONS

- ⬈ 55 x 85 mm
- ▭ Spicers Paper Stephen Uncoated 330gsm
- ✎ CMYK
- ✳ Digital print

The potential redesign of Japanese bookstore, Kinokuniya, was based upon the mixed harmony visualised in the store's simplistic and natural design. Fusing the letter 'K' with an opened book, the custom typeface and logo in bright purple gradation epitomised the life and energy you can find in books.

012

SPECIFICATIONS

- ⬈ 55 x 90 mm
- ▭ Toku A Cushion 1mm
- ✎ 2 PMS
- ✳ Hot stamp

A new name was conceived for the graphic design house and the new identity with the name 'COMMUNE' was originated from their fundamental belief in "Do something fun and make someone mouth water". The word 'COMMUNE' was picked to impart an addition closeness to the meaning of 'community'.

013

SPECIFICATIONS

- ⤢ 90 x 50 mm
- ▯ Sirio White 350gsm
- ✎ CMYK
- ✳ Foil block (Black), Die-cut

Sarah Davies was regarded the 'best-looking' client by Couple. The forward slash ' / ' was used as a simple visual statement to accentuate her multiple capabilities of being a TV presenter 'slash' master of Ceremonies 'slash' ambassador 'slash' model.

014

SPECIFICATIONS

- ⤢ 31.8 x 88.9 mm
- ▯ Neenah Classic Crest 150gsm
- ✎ CMYK
- ✳ Clear varnish, Foil block

Let's get it surprisingly straightforward – by saying 'hi' with your mouth and on the card, Megan Cummins concealed that elephant in the room with a little interactive entertainment to make her introduction memorable. The covering-up layer was actually a cost-effective substitute for the costly scratch-off ink. The trick was done by stamping the message with a clear varnish and a layer of foil with the help of Brunner Printing.

015

SPECIFICATIONS

- ⤢ 50 x 90 mm
- ▯ 2 versions: B & W Matt Paper 350gsm
- ✎ CMYK
- ✳ Screenprint

Young Moscow architectural bureau, Arch Idea, was looking for a clean yet flexible logo for creative variations, and a simple square was resulted as the mix of speech bubble and the firm's expertise in architecture and interior design. It also serves as a module that can be multiplied to form text blocks as side rooms in stationery layouts.

016

SPECIFICATIONS

- ⤢ 50 x 90 mm
- ▯ Cartboard 370gsm
- ✎ CMYK
- ✳ -

Just Moved provides full, low-cost local and national residential moving services in Canada, and its identity was principally made economical to realise, to accent the practicality and ease of movement with Just Moved. Minimal decorations and prints were applied, with circles and arrow indicating the change of address like a quick handwritten remark drawn with a black marker pen. The logo layout changes accordingly to the media such as stationery and uniforms.

017

SPECIFICATIONS

- ⤢ 54 x 86 mm
- ▯ Mirriboard Argent 365gsm
- ✎ PMS Black
- ✳ -

Designer Demian Conrad considers himself a kind of 'coiffeur' who deals with clients with communication problems to solve, and he would help create meanings and make clients happy, just like what hairdressers do when they cut and shape clients' hair. The card comprises a mirror surface so you would know when you need a new haircut.

018

SPECIFICATIONS

- ⤢ 54 x 86 mm
- ▯ Mondo Offset 350gsm
- ✎ PMS Black
- ✳ -

Ideas just jump in your head when they emerge, so the card of Jazz musician and composer, Frank Salis, included two rolls of stave for improvised composition. It was also meant to be a sweet idea to convey customised tonal messages as a personalised introduction to anyone who is going to get the card.

019

SPECIFICATIONS

⤢ 55 x 85 mm

▯ Clear plastic
(Polycarbonate)

✎ Maraflex FX / FX 980 black

✳ Screenprint, Die-cut

Yaniz Merican is renowned for her art-ist management in the hip hop industry in the states, and her firm, YZ International, is now at the forefront of the Malaysian hip hop scene. YZ's corporate identity was brought together as a showcase for her ex-panding international artist roster. The clear polycarbonate business cards with black screenprints were produced for a du-rable look and feel.

020

SPECIFICATIONS

⤢ 90 x 52 mm

▯ Mirriboard Silver 270gsm

✎ CMYK

✳ Emboss

The shiny chrome was an interpretation of the studio's name — Heydays, and the card-board indicated 'function', 'everyday use' and 'storage' in their studio, casting a contrast to the chrome. The use of 'func-tion' is further elaborated in the heavy use of custom tape for labelling and address. Print finishing includes blind emboss, mir-ror board, cardboard and silkscreened jewel cases.

021

SPECIFICATIONS

⤢ 50.8 x 88.9 mm

▯ Neenah Classic Crest Avon
Brilliant White 352gsm

✎ PMS 426

✳ Clear Foil block

Standing on the Ludlow Street of New York, an important cultural street rich with history, Stella Filante is missioned to bring back the newest and most interesting designs hand-picked from around the world. The retrospective stencil type setting is a reflection of the neighbourhood and the shop's showcase. A clean modular pattern was applied to evoke a feminine and understated elegance of the brand.

022

SPECIFICATIONS

⤢ 90 x 54 mm

▯ New Gentle 250gsm

✎ PMS Black 7 U,
Cool Grey 9 U

✳ -

The Pawn is situated in a historical tene-ment building, recently revitalised as part of the heritage conservation policy in Hong Kong. The place was used to be a pawn shop, and the restaurant's name, fashionably em-braced in the traditional pawn shop sign, was taken to reflect this transition into this current hot spot for Western cuisine. Historical pictures relevant to the old-time business were added for a vintage style against the modern elements.

023

SPECIFICATIONS

⤢ 55 x 90 mm

▯ 1mm Technical Card 750gsm

✎ -

✳ Foil (Black), Deboss

Beautiful is about a different perception of things. Based on the idea 'Everything has its beauty, but not everyone sees it', the 'beauty' of troubles, challenges, chaos and death was illustrated on the back of the name cards and in the letterheads, asking everyone to remember the existence of posi-tive things in life. Stickers of strange animals were made to personalise the differ-ent envelopes to hand.

024

SPECIFICATIONS

⤢ 54 x 90 mm

▯ Aluminum foil

✎ Black

✳ Screenprint

'84000' means infinite possibility. Set up by Stanley Wong, better known as 'anothermoun-tainman', in 2007, 84000 is dedicated to a diversity of design services alongside pho-tography and fine arts. The unique crumples made by a simple squeeze is an attempt to enhance the spirit behind.

025

SPECIFICATIONS

- ⊡ 52 x 86 mm
- ▢ Scandia 2000 Uncoated Offset 60gsm
- ✎ CMYK
- ✳ Perforation, Bookbinding

Founded in 2002 and discontinued in 2005, UNIT- was an independent design studio based in Copenhagen, Denmark. Involved in divergent networks, from cultural life to social spaces and sub-culture, UNIT- developed ideas and concepts in intellectual, graphic, interior and industrial design. Evident in NR1391, you will know function always defines the form.

026

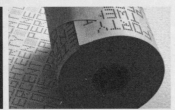

SPECIFICATIONS

- ⊡ 55 x 85 mm
- ▢ Knight Smooth White 350gsm
- ✎ PMS Black U
- ✳ -

Eighteen Percent is the photographic division of Sydney-based graphic design studio, Valentine Associates. The logo and alphabets were made to illustrate the qualities in both digital and analogue photography, with a custom-made typeface inspired by a recently processed negatives collection. The brand was carried throughout all stationery items, making way for a simple, fun and informative business card.

027

SPECIFICATIONS

- ⊡ 54 x 90 mm
- ▢ Blotting Paper 2mm
- ✎ PMS Black
- ✳ Hot stamp, Deboss

Estudio is a new photography studio which offers a list of professional services for rent in locations including Hong Kong and Shanghai. With a strong team of experts composed of art directors, make-up artists and administrators, etc, a template design was produced, compiling a flexible name card with blanks to fill in. The blind embossing indicating a service for rent forms a compelling impression that applies to any names written on the card.

028

SPECIFICATIONS

- ⊡ 50.8 x 88.9 mm
- ▢ Uncoated Stock (Partly recycled)
- ✎ 2 PMS
- ✳ -

Plania is an urban planning company. Playing on its mantra 'from the abstract to the concrete', a logo was designed to appear as scattered simple shapes with no meanings on one side, and the complete face of the company's name on the other. This deconstructive play was carried through Plania's stationery and printed paraphernalia. Marie-Hélène Trottier of Bleublancrouge had provided creative directions for the Plania card.

029

SPECIFICATIONS

- ⊡ 55 x 85 mm
- ▢ Woodfree Uncoated 300gsm
- ✎ -
- ✳ Emboss with fluorescent ink

Dreams Factory's name was printed with glow-in-the-dark ink with contact details blind-embossed on the back. It appears like a merely plain white card under bright light, but the studio's name would amazingly stand out when it is placed in the dark. Dreams Factory is a photography studio in Richmond, US.

030

SPECIFICATIONS

- ⊡ 50.8 x 88.9 mm
- ▢ Mohawk Superfine 130lb Double Thick Cover
- ✎ CMYK
- ✳ Letterpress

Stephen Burks and his studio, Readymade Projects, have been doing creative directions and industrial design for retail interiors, events among other disciplines. A new identity was developed to refresh Readymade's face. A set of six dynamic logos was generated with marks, symbols, signs and spacing taking the vowel's places. The coded brand name was renovated with a set of new year icons on the studio's new year card.

031

SPECIFICATIONS

- 95 × 95 mm
- Absorbent Coaster Paper 1.5mm (Coaster), Natural Offset 300gsm (Box)
- PMS Warm Grey 1 U, Warm Grey 2 U, Black 2 U
- –

Antrepo Design Industry believes that, like the way the world is constructed, Antrepo is composed of four basic elements, namely air, water, earth, and fire. Resembling the chemical symbols displayed in the periodic table, the name 'Antrepo' was dissected and printed on the coasters, as 'An' for Analysis (element of research), 'Tr' for Translatum (element of structure), 'E' for Eccentric (element of uniqueness), 'Po' for Positus (element of freshness).

032

SPECIFICATIONS

- 55 × 90 mm
- Spicers Stephen Swiss White 280gsm
- PMS 8623
- Letterpress

Five lines of the musical stave, punctuated by a heavier sixth has added up to the number of strings on a guitar, concluding Daniel Calabro's profession as a guitarist or guitar teacher. The visual-pun was beautifully letterpressed into a highly tactile stock for an instantly alluring and memorable result.

033

SPECIFICATIONS

- 90 × 55 mm
- Superfine Eggshell Ultra White 352gsm
- PMS Black 7 U
- Gunmetal Foil block

Chuan Pictures is a new production company set up by Singapore auteur Royston Tan. Rendered in a custom sans-serif typeface and encapsulated within a rising droplet, the character 'chuan', meaning 'fountain' in Chinese, celebrates simplicity and balances tradition with modernity, stability and dynamism on the name cards. The design repeats on the address stickers customised letterheads.

034

SPECIFICATIONS

- 90 × 50 mm
- Naturalis Smooth Finish Soft White 330gsm
- PMS 425 U, 1595 U
- Die-cut, Emboss

The new mark for the General Insurance Association of Singapore was designed to balance tradition with future needs. With the corporate orange tone muted and paired with an elegant modern typeface to reflect maturity, the ascending letters suggest depth and growth in the design. The two enclosing circles were merged to symbolise dynamic unity between the industry and association.

035

SPECIFICATIONS

- 90 × 55 mm
- Van neuveau 209gsm
- 2 PMS
- –

Sapporo-based theatrical team, INADA GUMI, believes acting is all about throwing away your original identity and being another self through body movements, facial expressions and your tones and words. INADA GUMI's logo functions the same way – punctuations and strokes adopted from English alphabet system, recognised by its serif and loop, were pulled out to construct the Japanese Katakana and Kanji for the group.

036

SPECIFICATIONS

- 55 × 90 mm
- Satogami 209gsm
- 2 PMS
- –

A-TO is a table ware shop in Nara, Japan, and the name 'A-TO' was picked for a pure gratitude, like the way children pronounce 'thank you' in the area. The shop logo was made based on the shape of a serving dish, so the dish would be thanking you in a lovingly way.

037

SPECIFICATIONS

- ⤢ 55 x 85 mm
- ▢ Fedrigoni Century Cottone Wowe White Uncoated 180gsm
- ✎ CMYK
- ✳ Digital print, Markerpen

Members of Playzebra Magazine's editorial staff are theoretically entitled to the same card with everybody's name and contact methods listed out in a row. The staff members are invited to customise their own card by crossing other people's personal data out and retaining their own.

038

SPECIFICATIONS

- ⤢ 55 x 85 mm
- ▢ 361L Stainless Steel
- ✎ -
- ✳ Laser etch

Metal is a very common material for orthopaedic surgery, both in transplants and surgical apparatus, so these little stainless steel panels were used to bring out the feel. The clean and modern touch of steel was juxtaposed with classical typography, suggesting the history and heritage of the profession itself. .

039

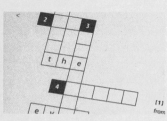

SPECIFICATIONS

- ⤢ 85 x 55 mm
- ▢ Couché Matt 350gsm
- ✎ CMYK
- ✳ Screenprint, UV Varnish

Formed to experiment new forms of approaching light and architecture as a whole, get a light incarnates their guiding principles with luminescent gloss (UV varnish), inviting clients to start experiencing the art from its business card and communication materials. The black rectangles were alluding to the architectural space and darkness in space.

040

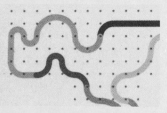

SPECIFICATIONS

- ⤢ 85 x 55 mm
- ▢ Nopaset Uncoated 300gsm
- ✎ CMYK
- ✳ -

Tallaght Community Arts is the platform to connect local community through creativity. A simple grid of dots with colourful illustrations forms a bright image for the group while revealing itself as a supporting framework for creativity. The logo 'T' is to be displayed in classes and exhibitions and printed on postcards.

041

SPECIFICATIONS

- ⤢ 85 x 55 mm
- ▢ Cyclus Offset 300gsm
- ✎ PMS Black 7
- ✳ -

Founded and curated by Dan Witchell of Proud Creative, Kemistry Gallery is a small independent gallery dedicated to the exhibition of work by outstanding designers. A neat and simple monochromatic identity was intended to let the artists' works shine.

042

SPECIFICATIONS

- ⤢ 55 x 85 mm
- ▢ GF Smith Ebony Colourplan 1400gsm
- ✎ -
- ✳ Foil block (White)

Creative directors at B&W Studio, Lee Bradley and Steve Wills, i.e. B&W and hence Black & White, had produced this identity for their own idea factory. Surrounding the mono-tone idea, information was foil blocked onto the Ebony Colourplan with the subtly printed letterhead on the reverse and displayed just when the light shown through. Black-and-white images were used in their brochures to coordinate the theme.

SPECIFICATIONS

- 🗗 85 x 55 mm
- 🗋 Conqueror Brilliant White Wove 350gsm
- ✏ PMS Black
- ✴ --

Russell Marsh casts models for fashion shows and photo shoots, and spotting perfection and distinctive qualities is what he does best. The most perfect and beautiful proportions of golden section was applied to allude to his expertise. No concrete logo was designed for this project.

SPECIFICATIONS

- 🗗 90 x 55 mm
- 🗋 Spicers Speldergel 350gsm
- ✏ CMYK
- ✴ Spot foil

Atypical online vintage rag seller 'Claire Incorruptible' needed an overhaul of their branding, and Mash wanted to create a brand identity with more sophistication. A timeless feel was needed, less the boring with the obvious vintage feel. An illustrated pattern was born with the use of double hit black ink combined with areas of spot foiling.

SPECIFICATIONS

- 🗗 54 x 90 mm
- 🗋 White Card Stock 300gsm
- ✏ PMS Black
- ✴ Varnish

The task was to develop a new identity for a small bookshop in London's East End, so Mihaylov came up with two quotation marks to hint at the inspiring quotes which you would come across as you read. The marks are monograms for the shop's initial, 'E' and 'B'.

SPECIFICATIONS

- 🗗 85 x 55 mm
- 🗋 Conqueror Diamond White Wove 350gsm
- ✏ PMS Black
- ✴ Spot UV

Paramount Private Members' Club is situated on the top floors of Centre Point, one of the earliest skyscrapers in London, and the trio-colour identity was made to honour the raw aesthetics in the Brutalist architecture and op art, also from the 1960s. The notion of height was reflected in the upward moments in the gradation patterns, with a greyscale to denote the concrete façade in a very subtle tone.

SPECIFICATIONS

- 🗗 55 x 85 mm
- 🗋 Colourplan Nero 350gsm
- ✏ -
- ✴ Foil block (White)

Brighton modern furniture and accessories retailer, The Lollipop Shoppe, was opening a new retailer shop in London and starting their own product line. The stencil typeface is integral to the identity, contributing a physical description for the real objects they offer in store. A sense of heritage and sophistication is embodied in a straightforward manner like how Lollipop runs its shop.

SPECIFICATIONS

- 🗗 44.5 x 88.9 mm
- 🗋 Black Royal Compliments 541gsm Duplex
- ✏ -
- ✴ Engrave (White), Die-cut

When it came to the design for his own business card, art director and graphic designer, Alan Valek, wanted a minimal look in appearance but unorthodox texture when his potential clients touch the card. The Black Royal Compliments® Paper was picked for its antique vellum finish, with die-cut round corners and white engraving on both sides of the card.

049

SPECIFICATIONS

- ⤢ 80 x 55 mm
- ▭ Sarriópapel Supralbor Blanco 315gsm
- ✎ CMYK
- ❋ Spot UV, Varnish

The owner's modern creed in running a different cocktail bar was incorporated in the brand 'I+Drink' inspired by the abbreviation of 'research and development', i.e. R+D or I+D by Spanish means. The project comprised corporate identity, architectural and graphic formulation, alongside product design for the modules, lamps, beer tap and glassware for cocktails. Humorous connotations were rolled out in all touch points to explicate the brand's soul.

050

SPECIFICATIONS

- ⤢ 55 x 85 mm
- ▭ St. Cotton Plain 300gsm
- ✎ PMS 440 U
- ❋ Clear Foil block

Constantly scouting around for eyewears from around the world, the optical boutique is represented by a logotype that alludes to the workings of human eye, like the inversion of light rays through the lens. The identity also tests your vision with the play of light and tactile feedback - if you fail to make out the logo with the naked eye, it is the time for your to check your eyes.

051

SPECIFICATIONS

- ⤢ 60 x 95 mm
- ▭ Fine Paper 209gsm
- ✎ CMYK
- ❋ Laser-cut, Die-cut

MIXTAPE GENERATION is a personal design project of Koji Sueyoshi who is enthusiastic about digging interesting things from different culture and place. The MIXTAPE GENERATION business card is a visualisation of Sueyoshi's project, so as the starting point of his designer life.

052

SPECIFICATIONS

- ⤢ 55 x 85 mm
- ▭ Spicers Freelife Smooth White 320gsm
- ✎ CMYK
- ❋ Thermography (Black)

Carla Grbac works predominantly at a large loom, weaving rows of thread around the reeds to form her pieces. Graphically associating her name to the weaving, raised impressions were produced to resemble the patterns and texture composed by the warp and weft. The black-and-white akin to weaving diagrams palette ties in with the minimal colours in Grbac's fabric.

053

SPECIFICATIONS

- ⤢ 51 x 89 mm
- ▭ Couché 230gsm
- ✎ CMYK
- ❋ Matt lamination, Hot stamp (Gold)

Malota is the pseudonym of Mar Hernandez, where Malotaprojects is a multi-disciplinary study on projects of illustration, design and animation. The featuring business cards and postcards were designed by Malota herself to her creative instinct with a professional touch.

054

SPECIFICATIONS

- ⤢ 55 x 85 mm
- ▭ GF Smith Bagdad Brown Colourplan 270gsm
- ✎ -
- ❋ Foil block (Gold)

Graphic Bar is a bar in Golden Square of London, the goal of this project was to simply reflect the bar's name in the design. The creative process was a very quick one, and the identity remained experimental, reminiscent of the days of old in the graphic profile like when one was at university playing around with type and composition.

055

SPECIFICATIONS

⤢ 90 x 50 mm

▯ Toku-A-cushion 0.6mm 335gsm

✒ CMYK, Silver

✳ Hot stamp

The key idea in Futaba.'s works is 'Life, Nature, and Technology', and they would very much want to make their business cards special for its recipients. Applying the technique of printing press foil on the vein skeleton of the plant, the fern shines like glittering jewels and delicate texture appealing to you visually and by means of touch.

056

SPECIFICATIONS

⤢ 90 x 55 mm

▯ Mr. A 209gsm

✒ 1 PMS

✳ Screenprint

This card was produced for Takuto Ko-sukegawa who has now moved to live and work in Tokyo. The raised frame in the centre of the card was borrowed from the useful references that a photographer would come across while they shoot.

057

SPECIFICATIONS

⤢ 55 x 85 mm

▯ GF Smith Naturalis Absolute White Matt 330gsm

✒ PMS Black

✳ Foil block (Silver)

El Studio created the brand identity for KLJ Solutions, an independent specialist consultancy, working in partnership with business to evaluate and maintain structured strategies. The print and silver foiling were applied onto refined crafted stocks to accentuate the client's precise and concise approach to business evaluation.

058

SPECIFICATIONS

⤢ 90 x 50 mm

▯ Maple White 250gsm

✒ PMS Black U

✳ Die-cut

L'escalier is an art studio-cum-boutique in Singapore. The brandmark is the ab-straction of a staircase's cross section, resulting in a ʌ-like logo that could mutate into super graphics to dress up the shop. An enlarged version of the logo was produced as store-cards or swing-tags. A corner of the business card is sniffed off to accent the logo's silhouette over the super white stock.

059

SPECIFICATIONS

⤢ 85 x 55 mm

▯ GF Smith Colourplan 270gsm Duplex

✒ PMS 168 U

✳ Foil block (Copper)

Acupuncturist Shareen Kalideen wanted an elegant logo without a hint of new age nonsense, and Magpie responded by getting the design straight to the point. A real celebration of acupuncture, the copper foil monogram references the needles that Kali-deen use for her practice, with the back-ground colour portraying skin tones.

060

SPECIFICATIONS

⤢ 90 x 55 mm

▯ Antalis Magno Satin White 300gsm

✒ PMS 8581, 8623

✳ Overprint

Willowlamp is the brainchild of Johan-nesburg-based design duo 'TeamTwo', Adam Hoets and Sian Eliot. It is the name of the team's maiden product range of custom designed lights. These cards are authenti-cally showcasing the South African-inspired chandeliers to the international interior design stage.

061

SPECIFICATIONS

- ⬚ 50.8 x 88.9 mm
- ▦ Balsa wood
- ✒ -
- ✳ Black laser on a Xerox 250 colour printer

The winning entry in ADCMW Real Show contest 2009 was a logo and stationery set designed to reflect the modularity and friendliness of 925 Furniture's self-assembly hardwood furniture line. The logo, separable into three modular panels, was printed on a very light and soft hardwood, balsa, varied in a range of stains and finishes available in store. Diagrams were attached to illustrate the different methods for constructing '925 blocks'.

062

SPECIFICATIONS

- ⬚ 50 x 88 mm
- ▦ Walnut Veneer 430gsm
- ✒ -
- ✳ Laser-cut, Engrave

Fifth Floor is a creative space where Robert Apodaca intersects art, design and architecture design projects with focuses on the simplicity of form, economy of materials and elegance in approach. The cards are laser-cut and engraved from various wood veneers remnant from furniture projects. The wooden cards also serve to sample the materials of which many of the design objects at Fifth Floor are created.

063

SPECIFICATIONS

- ⬚ 50.8 x 88.9 mm
- ▦ French Paper Company Construction Fuse Green 100lb
- ✒ CMYK
- ✳ Digital print, Sticker

Ellie Snow has handmade these cards to catch a conference where she could introduce her design blog 'Mint'. Thinking of incorporating DIY elements into the card with the idea of mix-and-match, Snow gave her cards a delicate pattern with a variety of Japanese masking tapes on two colour stock left over from past projects. A string was responding to her blog's readers who mentioned reading her entries was like getting a 'gift' from her every day.

064

SPECIFICATIONS

- ⬚ 50.8 x 177.8 mm (Open), 50.8 x 88.9 mm (Closed)
- ▦ Pegasus Brilliant White Smooth Cover 432gsm
- ✒ PMS 4625 U
- ✳ Scoring

Specialising in brand identity, Paprika demonstrates their mastery over their own stationery system where information is treated as a design on a recurring theme. Almost like a trompe l'oeil, the result was a bar code indicating the studio's vision and approach.

065

SPECIFICATIONS

- ⬚ 148 x 104 mm (Open), 74 x 52 mm (Closed)
- ▦ Kraftpaper 80gsm
- ✒ CMYK
- ✳ Screenprint (Phosphorescent ink)

Bendita Gloria is a Barcelona-based design duo who loves small costumers and is not afraid of big ones. Clean and their names are endowed with its own light of the phosphorescent ink.

066

SPECIFICATIONS

- ⬚ 55 x 85 mm
- ▦ Mandarin Colourplan 540gsm
- ✒ CMYK, PMS 179 C
- ✳ Foil block

Low Winter Sun is a consultancy specialising in third sector marketing and community-based research work. Its clients include OXFAM and the Department for Energy and Climate Change. The nature of the practice was celebrated with the sharp contrast between mandarin Colourplan stock and thick foil-blocked letters. The principle font was the solid and condensed Placard, creating a balance of impact and professionalism with the elegant serif font.

067

SPECIFICATIONS

⬈ 50 x 90 mm

🗎 Tom & Otto Silk 350gsm

✒ PMS Cool Grey 11 C

✳ Screenprint

The English meaning for Blusyne is `flea'. It might not be a mouth-watering name for a restaurant, but it is the deli owner's lovely dog's name, and now a term for 'a cosy place'. The zestful doggy logo appears on a range of items, including matchboxes, coasters and the check.

068

SPECIFICATIONS

⬈ 420 x 297 mm

🗎 Speicers Stephen Eggshell 320gsm

✒ CMYK

✳ Perforation

Burn Cottage practises biodynamics in their winery, a mystical practice founded by Rudolf Steiner who was heavily influenced by the writings of Johann Wolfgang Von Goethe. Looking for the hands-on characteristics in the brand, Mash created a collage with one of Goethe's fairy tale, 'The Green Snake and the Beautiful Lily'. The images were printed into a perforated poster which can be torn apart into individual business cards.

069

SPECIFICATIONS

⬈ 55 x 90 mm

🗎 KW Doggett Expressions Super Smooth 350gsm

✒ CMYK

✳ -

Behind this identity is a romantic story of the happily-married heads of Thirdrow Films meeting each other for the first time in the third row of a local cinema. The row of seats was the key ingredient made to embrace and integrate the lovely sentiment into each of Thirdrow Films' new culturally-inspired productions. The chairs were outlined to give a coordinating look on the clients' name cards.

070

SPECIFICATIONS

⬈ 85 x 55 mm

🗎 Bankpost 90gsm

✒ CMYK

✳ -

Based on the idea of 'you complete me', an identity collection for photographer Muriel Mager contains a set of three stationery items that would assemble the practitioner's own work. The picture was printed in varied tones to separate the items.

071

SPECIFICATIONS

⬈ 55 x 85 mm

🗎 -

✒ -

✳ Various

Masking a variation of printing effects into the three characters of the client's initial, the proposing corporate identity is like a little sample demonstrating their printers' performance on little cards or in the letterhead. Each of the characters comes with 16 designs, composing hundreds of varieties for the client's look.

072

SPECIFICATIONS

⬈ 55 x 85 mm

🗎 ProMail Plus 300gsm

✒ PMS Rhodamine Red U, Orange 021 U, 298 U, 367 U

✳ -

Founded in 2004 and owned by Pieter van Rosmalen of CakeLab, CakeType specialises in the design, production and distribution of original typefaces. A custom 'pattern' typeface is specially developed with a vector-based font, weaving the vivid fun in type design.

073

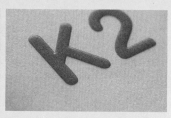

SPECIFICATIONS

- ⬚ 90 x 55 mm
- ◰ Concept Vellum Smooth 352gsm
- ✎ PMS 5767 U
- ✳ Deboss

K2 is a boutique investment company based in New Zealand, and the client was looking for a clean but bold look that would appeal to investors with a not-so-corporate feel. The feeling of security and confidence were reassured on the card.

074

SPECIFICATIONS

- ⬚ 55 x 90 mm
- ◰ Knight Smooth 352gsm
- ✎ PMS 806 U
- ✳ Deboss, Foil block (Gold, Silver)

Crazy, colourful and memorable, the logotype for Yvonne Moxham's production practice, 'Left Brain Right', merged the first letters of the three words as one element sitting in the middle of the card. The application of debossed foil over the shocking pink stock has let the logo shine in an effortless way.

075

SPECIFICATIONS

- ⬚ 54 x 90 mm
- ◰ Matt Black Card 350gsm
- ✎ -
- ✳ Foil block (White), Die-cut

A little knowledge in Chinese might help to decode this abstract graphic, with strokes and structures attributing the enclosed parts of the Chinese character 'tu', denoting the last character of the designer's Chinese name. 'Tu' literally means 'graphics' and 'pictures', which he produces as a career. An arrow was die-cut on the edge was to signify Ng's name and contact details on the other side of the card.

076

SPECIFICATIONS

- ⬚ 55 x 85 mm
- ◰ Keaykolour Uncoated 300gsm
- ✎ PMS Cyan, Cool Grey 9
- ✳ -

ate has been quantitatively and qualitatively developed over the years, and thus a dynamic logo was composed to pass on these values with features of data charts. The logo was also intended to contrast the solemnness in ate's accounting and training practise in a calm and trustworthy mood.

077

SPECIFICATIONS

- ⬚ 55 x 88 mm
- ◰ Cyclus Offset Uncoated 300gsm
- ✎ CMYK
- ✳ -

The main objective of the rebranding of Airside was to communicate the design agency's unique ability to cover the variety of design disciplines they involve. A new Airside logo, which eventually expanded into a separate family of sliced logos derived from the animated versions, was designed, suggesting the theme of moving without moving. Cyclus Offset is an environmentally-friendly product produced from 100% post consumer de-inked waste.

078

SPECIFICATIONS

- ⬚ 50.8 x 88.9 mm
- ◰ Beckett Concept Mahogany 160# 432gsm
- ✎ Custom white
- ✳ Engrave

Anthropologist, museum curator and founder of Pravina, Diana Zlatanovski, seeks to preserve cultural artefacts for the power and history they possess, and stories of people they tell. Adhering to the Pravina values, Vik LLC created as much of the brand collateral as possible by hand. A unique and professional branding system was therefore brought to live with the use of silkscreen, hand embossers and hole-punches.

079

SPECIFICATIONS

⤢ 63.5 x 63.5 mm

⊡ Strathmore Writing Wove
Platinum White 130# Cover
352gsm

✐ CMYK

☀ -

Labs is a small Chicago-based interactive
design office that works with a large network of designers and developers worldwide.
In need of a fresh identity for immediate
recognition with longevity, a clean and modern logo was built to suggest the cellular
nature of their network. Around it is a stationery system that provides a classic and
timeless environment that would effectively
extend the half-life of the identity, giving
the brand a broader appeal.

080

SPECIFICATIONS

⤢ 55 x 55 mm (Shop card),
282 x 330 mm (Brand tag)

⊡ Art Card 380gsm

✐ CMYK, PMS 539 C

☀ Gloss lamination, Die-cut

Wooonderland is a fashion retail playground
set to appeal to the young and the bold.
Sharing a link to its sister store 'Actually...', Wooonderland took on the ellipses
and converted them into three prominent circles underneath the 'W'. The brandmark also
functions as fun clips for tagging magazine
pages, school notes or folders, weaving a
vivid personality for the boutique as well
as the merchandise it carries.

081

SPECIFICATIONS

⤢ 55 x 90 mm

⊡ Multidesign 400gsm

✐ PMS Black, 805

☀ Emboss

Committing to pushing themselves a-hundred-
and-one percent, Action+Service's identity
was totally devised on the definition of
their brand name. By introducing the never-
ending story telling with words and picto-
grams, each document appears different yet
speaking the same visual language itself.

082

SPECIFICATIONS

⤢ 55 x 85 mm

⊡ Knight Vellum 200gsm

✐ PMS Black U, 151 U

☀ -

29 Bikes is recently established to design
and manufacture limited edition custom-built
bicycles. The identity was inspired by the
Clarendon typeface's bracket that resembles
a cross-bar.

083

SPECIFICATIONS

⤢ 55 x 55 mm

⊡ Couché Matt 250gsm

✐ CMYK, Pantone 7478 C

☀ Plastic package

With pixel cubes integral to NEW WOK's visual identity, playful attitudes is evident
everywhere to whet your appetite! Detachable
bookmarkers from its postal cards, stages of
a bowl of noodles evolving into a heart of
love, and instructions to build an origami
with your paper mat - the noodle shop in
Lisbao tells you how you could discover fun
while you consume.

084

SPECIFICATIONS

⤢ 85 x 55 mm

⊡ GF Smith Colourplan
270gsm Duplex

✐ PMS Black U

☀ -

Springing up each evening after the vegetable market finishes its day, this impromptu
venue is instantly recognised by locals as
'The Vegetable Bar'. 'Making the most of the
roots', the identity captures its nightly
metamorphosis with the sillhouette of a
vegetable-cum-wine glass over a subdued noc-
turnal palette.

085

SPECIFICATIONS

- ⬚ 55 x 90 mm
- ▯ Grandeur Zen White 350gsm
- ✎ CMYK, PMS Black 7 U, 429 U, 505 U, 7527 U
- ✳ Foil block (Black)

XTRA is one of Singapore's foremost retailers of designer furnishings. Compared with the old arrangement of 'X•tra', the new logotype was more simplified, capitalised and spaced out. The new identity was designed to project a tasteful and serious persona of the shop, with the 'X' drawing its strength and inspiration from the contour in classic designs like the Eames La Chaise.

086

SPECIFICATIONS

- ⬚ 55 x 90 mm
- ▯ New Raglin Snow Paper 220gsm
- ✎ PMS 419 U, Custom metallic bronze
- ✳ Screenprint, Emboss

SILNT was approached by Distillery Studio for an overhaul of their brand identity. Aimed for a more classic and sophisticated look based on the original design, the complex logo was stripped down to its organic form, with blind-embossing subtly revealing the details of the logo on both sides of the card.

087

SPECIFICATIONS

- ⬚ 55 x 85 mm
- ▯ 3 Colourplan (270gsm, 350gsm and 270gsm)
- ✎ -
- ✳ Foil block (Silver, White), Triplexing

A logo and printed identity for financial adviser, Diane Gray-Smith. The business cards are triplexed with a streak of hot pink colourplan running through the middle layer. The logotype and contact info was foil-blocked on both sides of the card.

088

SPECIFICATIONS

- ⬚ 45 x 45 mm
- ▯ FIOCCARDI Material Paper Light Grey 800gsm
- ✎ PMS Black, Blue
- ✳ Spot UV

MGNERD by MAURO GRIFONI is turning to a young audience of cool and stylish Italians, and to synchronise the brand's image with its pure and simple style, the logo strictly plays on the neutrality and cleanliness of Helvetica packed in the colours of eclectic blue and black. Original colours of the packaging materials were adopted to coordinate the natural tone.

089

SPECIFICATIONS

- ⬚ 85 x 55 mm
- ▯ Precision 350gsm
- ✎ PMS 360
- ✳ -

Following her success with revered Australian fashion label Scanlan & Theodore, Fiona Scanlan established the children's wear label Big By Fiona Scanlan in 2005. The brand embraces imagination and fun from a child's perspective, and the logotype was made to communicate cleanly and simply, almost childlike, in application. Whimsical garden graphics playfully extends across big's stationery to the retail environment, and also the clothing itself.

090

SPECIFICATIONS

- ⬚ Various
- ▯ Recycled paper
- ✎ PMS Magenta U, 447 U, 3135 U
- ✳ -

Stimulating children who live with a creative little universe in mind, the branding of Limo_kids aims to suggest these little customers to have fun re-using their shopping bags and packaging after shopping at their store. The visuals feature a kind of endearing rawness in between the lines and types that connects with kids aged between one and five.

091

SPECIFICATIONS

⬔ 88.9 x 50.8 mm

▯ Mohawk Superfine Eggshell
352gsm

✎ PMS 368 M, 373 M, 7533 M

✳ -

Eat Innovations is a full-course consultancy for the marketing of consumer packaged
goods. Akin to picking the right forks for
the right restaurants, Eat brings tasty
ideas to the shelf with a menu of services
to usher product ideas from concepts to the
consumer perspectives and all points in between. The idea was clearly conveyed in the
logo, related to the name 'Eat' itself.

092

SPECIFICATIONS

⬔ 55 x 85 mm (Closed)

▯ GF Smith B & W Colourplan
Boards 270gsm Duplex

✎ CMYK

✳ Emboss

The key is to project the creative personality of Massive's two founding partners,
and a sense of fun is injected through a
fashionable shot of them holding balloons in
front of their faces. Massive is a creative
events agency based in London responsible
for the production of extravagant parties,
launches and events. The script font logo
represents the authority, quality and deca-
dence that would be associated with any Massive event or party.

093

SPECIFICATIONS

⬔ 45 x 90 mm

▯ Sovereign Offset Silk
Coated 300gsm

✎ PMS Yellow, 426

✳ Die-cut, Matt lamination

The competition in Australia's commercial
and hospitality furniture industry is fierce,
and a unique and bold identity would defi-
nitely help Insitu to stand out. The result
is a combination of distinct colour and
exaggerated forms, reflective of the style of
furniture and the many exclusive Australian
agencies it holds.

094

SPECIFICATIONS

⬔ 55 x 85 mm

▯ Knight Smooth White 350gsm

✎ PMS 291, 293 U

✳ -

The One That Got Away is a fish and chips
shop full of passion, strength and fun. For
its bold and solid appearance, Clarendon was
adopted and stencilised on the card. The
word 'Away' was moved 'away' from the main
body as a humorous twist.

095

SPECIFICATIONS

⬔ 55 x 86 mm

▯ Normal Fancy Paper Card
250gsm

✎ PMS Black, 806 U

✳ Die-cut

Rice 5 (Wu Dou Mi) was established to build
big ideas out of trivial things. Specialising in interactive web designs, Rice 5 made
augmented reality technology part of their
greetings, with a simple code on the card.
Key in the designated URL and hold the card
in front of your webcam - a virtual staff
member would pop and greet respectively,
with their personal motto in view.

096

SPECIFICATIONS

⬔ 55 x 85 mm

▯ Expression 400gsm

✎ 6 PMS

✳ Spot UV

Huddle Design is recently established to
offer lateral thinking and insightful char-
ismatic solutions to companies and corporate
clients, and the name 'Huddle' is to reso-
nate their energetic approaches and teamwork
when it comes to engineering work. Eight 'H'
are touching each other to resemble the name
'huddle', and solid vivid colours are added
to reflect their ethos of simplicity and confidence along with a simple, round type.

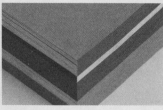

097

SPECIFICATIONS

- 50 x 75 mm
- Kraftboard 250gsm Duplex
- -
- Foil block (Black), Edge colouring (6 Colours)

A Friend Of Mine (AFOM.) is a small design practice run by Suzy Tuxen, who recalled the painstaking effort in realising the card design. With the help of a bookbinding specialist, the cards were clamped together and sanded on the edges before hand-sprayed with colours. Two sheets of kraft board were mounted for extra rigidity, with the colour combinations indicating 'business on the front, party on the sides'.

098

SPECIFICATIONS

- 57.2 x 79.4 mm (Closed)
- Mohawk Options True White 352gsm
- PMS 109, 314, 355, 420, 431, Custom red
- Foil block, Side gilding

Sarkissian Mason is a small idea-focused boutique committed to marketing with big ideas. Aiming for a face that shows confidence in handling big brands and large accounts, a visually-durable identity with great production details was created. The card set comes in six colours with glided edges.

099

SPECIFICATIONS

- 52 x 84 mm
- MAP Finland Scandia 2000 White 300gsm
- PMS Warm Red U, 102 U, 2925 U, 7481 U, Nova Star 777 Deep Space (Lint Group)
- Lacquer coating

Five companies specialising in five distinctive fields of interior design have gathered to operate under the umbrella of Vallila Interior. Hints of individual entities were intentionally avoided, resulted in a new unified look with simple colour bars to understate the body as a combination of allies.

100

SPECIFICATIONS

- 55 x 85 mm
- Colourplan 270gsm
- CMYK, PMS 802
- -

Guildford-based music project, Radar, is launched to unearth young talents that are off the radar, and the heart of the identity shows a bold illustration of throbbing pulse that evokes the notion of a radar. The colourful and flexible typographic approach is applied to create an eye-catching and vibrant hacker-esque identity which maps the locations of the activities at the centre point of the pulse.

101

SPECIFICATIONS

- 85 x 55 mm
- Pachica Paper 233gsm
- PKM 76, 226
- Foil block, Deboss

'Pachica' is a special Japanese paper which becomes translucent when hot-stamped, and the special feature inspired designer Yuko Uemura, who has a strong passion for silkscreen prints and colourful patterns for kitchen products and accessories. The tear drop shapes resemble the drops of inks that fall on her fabrics or cloth.

102

SPECIFICATIONS

- 55 x 85 mm
- Self-coloured Colourplan 350gsm
- -
- Foil block (Gold)

St George's Crypt is a Christian homeless charity based in Leeds. With focus retained on the church and its mission to help the disadvantaged, a letterhead was made simple but precious with gold foil, like its missions, on self-coloured business cards and envelopes.

103

SPECIFICATIONS

- ⬈ 50.8 x 88.9 mm
- 📄 Strathmore 130lb Double Thick Cover
- ✏️ CMYK
- ✳️ Letterpress, Edge colouring (4 Colours)

STUDIOCO is a design collective and a conclave for connection and compilation based in New York. The edges of their business cards were sprayed in alternative colours to signify these correlations between their design and its clients.

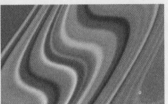

104

SPECIFICATIONS

- ⬈ 55 x 85 mm
- 📄 Opale 250gsm
- ✏️ PMS Red 032, 425
- ✳️ Edge colouring

EspaceFine is dedicated to the conception and realisation of cultural events and, as a curator, their role is to 'frame' the artists' work before presenting them to the public. This identity was a direct expression of this simple idea.

105

SPECIFICATIONS

- ⬈ 90 x 55 mm
- 📄 Antalis Magno Satin White 300gsm
- ✏️ CMYK
- ✳️ Spot foil

OIL stands for Original Insight Learning, a research company in the marketing communications industry who has been using physical analogy in the names of paraphernalia, such as oil cans and dipsticks. Distinctive patterns of iridescence alludes to a rainbow of subject matters from where viewers or researchers could mine insight with greater curiosity and excitement than grease.

106

SPECIFICATIONS

- ⬈ 90 x 110 mm (Open), 90 x 55 mm (Closed)
- 📄 Spicers Starblack 216gsm
- ✏️ PMS 877, 8222
- ✳️ Forme-cut

The initials of Chris Chen are merged to bring about this unique two-fold business card, which unfolds to unveil a simple black bold frame that helps to spot the extraordinary, like the way the photographer perceives the world. Clients are invited to lift the card and get a closer view of their familiar surrounding.

107

SPECIFICATIONS

- ⬈ 55 x 80 mm
- 📄 Blue Glow Edge Acrylic Plastic
- ✏️ PMS Cyan, 032
- ✳️ Laser-cut, Etching, Screenprint

Wigwam events is a group of space specialists and party designers with its core business covering lighting and event design, and the provision of bespoke accessories for marquee and non-marquee events. The new identity is dominated by a funky, dynamic typeface made form geometric shapes. The cards come in two version, on paper and plastic cards.

108

SPECIFICATIONS

- ⬈ 55 x 88 mm
- 📄 Neon Stock, Beermat Board, Greyboard
- ✏️ CMYK
- ✳️ Letterpress

Independent designer G-MAN is crazy about 1950's Americana. Starting his own design practice with his nickname at school, he designed these name cards to represent himself as 'an individual self-employed designer who is a bit different from the norm'. The bright and punk neon add a sense of urgency in getting to know G-MAN.

SPECIFICATIONS

- ⊠ 55 x 88 mm
- 🗋 Luxury Matt Board, Beermat Board
- ✎ CMYK
- ✳ Letterpress

Founded by G-MAN and photographer Lee Garland, Loose Collective is a group of six creatives specialising in offer photography, graphic design, website design/production, multi-media/video and Public Relations. The logo represents the idea of different elements coming together to form one thing.

SPECIFICATIONS

- ⊠ 55 x 85 mm
- 🗋 Fine Paper Conqueror Uncoated 250gsm
- ✎ CMYK, PMS 806
- ✳ Hot stamp (Black)

This identity reflects a brand in motion with dreamy rhythms. The geometrics and techno graphics in shapes of rays were aimed for a fresh and sonic touch to connect with the production of music and sound.

SPECIFICATIONS

- ⊠ 85 x 55 mm
- 🗋 Lenticular Printing Paper 300gsm
- ✎ CMYK
- ✳ Lenticular printing

Illustrating the growth of each staff member at The Creative Method staff and, more importantly, the studio's development, these business cards introduce the creative brains one by one. Lenticular printing was used to exhibit the transition between the staff's infant and adult look.

SPECIFICATIONS

- ⊠ 55 x 85 mm
- 🗋 Torras Papel Uncoated Matt Paper 350gsm
- ✎ PMS Black
- ✳ -

Encompassing movies and TV programmes, AL-GUIENVOLO aims at searching, developing and making productions in different audio-visual formats to suit different media. Appearing a bit like a piece of op art, the production house's name was dissolved in a panel of thin stripes flickering in black and white.

SPECIFICATIONS

- ⊠ 55 x 85 mm
- 🗋 Uncoated Stock 380gsm
- ✎ PMS 012 U, 426 U
- ✳ Die-cut

ISIS Productions wanted a complete re-brand and the brief was to create an identity that is as rich, bold and iconic, just as the artists and music it documents. The brand mark aims to appeal to their existing clients so as to attract more contemporary artists. The bold logo and brand colours create a versatile set of marks, patterns and typography to play with their stationery items and business cards.

SPECIFICATIONS

- ⊠ 85 x 50 mm
- 🗋 Duplexed Colourplan Pristine White 700gsm
- ✎ PMS Black 6 U, 485 U
- ✳ -

Sounding like where you could style your hair and shave beard, Barbershop is actually a music and sound design company set up by a quartet of influential music makers with diverse musical backgrounds. The musical instruments and colour stripes typical on the barber's pole seamlessly work together to relate their name with what they exactly produce.

115

SPECIFICATIONS

- 55 x 85 mm
- Greyboard 500gsm
- Luxor 391 Blue
- Foil block

Understanding how difficult it is to impress a stranger with concrete memories, this Dutch design studio helps its holders to remember with a simple and precise description of who they are. Just read the sentence aloud, which literally means 'You know that design agency with that difficult name' in English.

116

SPECIFICATIONS

- 55 x 90 mm
- Munken Polar 350gsm
- CMYK
- -

Laboratory is where discovery and experiments occur everyday, like Laboratorio, where new ideas breed as the result of originality and communication work. With genuineness, fascination and enthusiasm the key, every asset in the agency is all masked up in a laboratory fashion, evident in the colour and optimism.

117

SPECIFICATIONS

- 50 x 85 mm, 50 x 75 mm, 50 x 220 mm
- Munken Pure 300gsm, Magno Satin White 300gsm
- CMYK, 7 PMS
- Overprint, Spot foil, Emboss, Spot UV, Digital print, Laser-cut

Specialising in strategic brand development with design, REX Company Compendium features a concise profile of the company as well as a collection of project case studies and selected articles. The company card comes in a collection of four designs, distinctive in their stock, dimensions and finishing, embracing the principles and beliefs they bear while they create.

118

SPECIFICATIONS

- 450 x 90 mm (Open), 55 x 90 mm (Closed)
- Stephen Swiss White 330gsm
- CMYK, 1 PMS
- Perforation

A vibrant picture mark referencing the process of architecture was physically built on the geometric principals of tesseracts. The way that architecture interacts with our surroundings was conveyed through the shooting of banal environments with the symbolic inclusion of human participation and dynamics presented by the different looks of the mark. The travelogue-like picture series was set to amuse in form of a perforated business-card train.

119

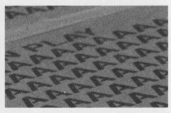

SPECIFICATIONS

- 85 x 55 mm
- Torras Papel Uncoated Matt Paper 350gsm
- Fluorescent red & black
- -

EL YA is a sound recording studio for advertising, and its name conveys the literal meaning of 'right now' in English. Expanding the YA-word in a never-ending manner, the business cards express an urgent request, like "call me right nooooooooooooooooooooow". It also composes an exciting yell, responding to the studio's practice in the most quiet form.

120

SPECIFICATIONS

- 85 x 55 mm
- Torras Papel Uncoated Matt paper 350gsm
- PMS Black
- -

The English translation for 5°PINO is "Fifth Pine". The graphics for the identity are rooted in a story about a forest, where pines grow and live. An organic theme is dispersed around the bar and restaurant's stationery in a natural finish.

121

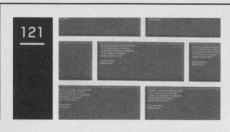

SPECIFICATIONS

- ⬚ 43 x 95 mm
- 🗋 Colourplan Mist with Granular embossed effect 350gsm
- ✏ PMS 165 U
- ✳ Emboss, Perforation

The reddish brick wall would be a direct allusion to the construction industry that Machells Building Contractors involve. The brick texture is embossed in shapes of blocks and seperated by perforation, allowing users to tear off the cards when needed.

122

SPECIFICATIONS

- ⬚ 55 x 75 mm
- 🗋 Keaykolour Recycled Black 400gsm
- ✏ -
- ✳ Foil block (Gold)

Cream is a director-based boutique production company and it represents some of the finest directors in Australia and North America. The goal of this project was to create an identity that projects attitude with a contemporary feel. The use of gold foiling throughout the collateral added an air of quality to the identity and the boutique nature of the production house. Keaykolour Recycled Black is 75% produced from recycled fibre using ECF.

123

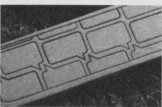

SPECIFICATIONS

- ⬚ 25.4 x 152.4 mm
- 🗋 Wooden Tongue Depressor
- ✏ PMS Black U
- ✳ Letterpress

Matt Van Ekeren's tongue depressors are his initial material proof of his 'playful and insightful solutions...infused with educated humour' to a total stranger. Containing simple contact details and layers of thoughts and speech, the letterpress 'cards' are suggestive of his role as a 'problem solver' on creative directions, motion and print designs, so as his pseudonym, 'design that talks'.

124

SPECIFICATIONS

- ⬚ 85.6 x 54 mm
- 🗋 White Polished Cardboard 1000gsm
- ✏ -
- ✳ Laser-cut, Engrave

1scale1's urgent need of a new business card design for an upcoming conference just came upon the landing of their new laser-cutter, resulting in the dynamic man figure bearing their contact details on their torsos. The little man and his parts were not entirely cut through – clients could just give a little press, pop the figures out and create their own panel-man to stand on their desk.

125

SPECIFICATIONS

- ⬚ 55 x 90 mm
- 🗋 Spicers Stephen 320gsm
- ✏ CMYK
- ✳ Foil block (Gold)

A set of swing tags and business cards was produced for Pipsqueek in Saigon's new retail store which is dedicated to bringing vintage fashion to modern life. Besides the use of bulky recycled paper stock with four colour printing and gold foil, the swing tags were drenched for a crumpled look and ragged feel.

126

SPECIFICATIONS

- ⬚ 70 x 54 mm (Irregular)
- 🗋 Uncoated Art Paper 280gsm
- ✏ CMYK
- ✳ Engrave, Spot UV

Using a self-portrait as the key visual and a short self-introduction in a paragraph-like dialogue between the audience and herself, the freelance photographer, writer and stylist talks her character directly on the card. Red lines were hand-drawn on the card to highlight important contact details so as a sense of personal approach.

127

SPECIFICATIONS

⤢ 80 x 50 mm

🗋 Matt Art Card 200gsm

🖊 CMYK

☀ Die-cut

Some say 'simple is happiness', and from Loo's business card, you can tell he is a guy who lives a simple, joyful life. Loo's initial 'D' was die-cut into the card, forming a smiling character itself.

128

SPECIFICATIONS

⤢ 85 x 54 mm

🗋 Cyclus Offset 170gsm

🖊 CMYK, PMS 875 C

☀ Special ink (Bronze)

DSAA is a postgraduate art degree course at Olivier de Serres. Bringing in the energy and enthusiasm for design in student from different disciplines, this winning design produced in 2007 invited students to play around and photographed with letter blocks spelling the degree's name. The project included a poster, a printed and digital invitation as well as business cards for the students.

129

SPECIFICATIONS

⤢ 55 x 85 mm

🗋 Fedrigoni Century Cottone Wowe White Uncoated 180gsm

🖊 CMYK

☀ Digital print

Originated from the embarrassing moments when you have nothing to write on besides your sweating palms when people exchange contacts, these are the very "personal-ised" business card for ZEBRA's staff. Each card features a hand of the design agency's individual staff bearing their personal contacts in their own handwriting on their palms. The person's body and feet were also photographed for an genuine first-person top view.

130

SPECIFICATIONS

⤢ 50 x 90 mm

🗋 Expression Super Smooth Uncoated 350gsm

🖊 -

☀ Hand stamp with regular black ink stamp pad

Sassen Design is a Melbourne design studio that loves getting ink onto paper. Deceptively bold and rustic, the studio's name and contact details were crafted and stamped gingerly onto the cards by hands.

131

SPECIFICATIONS

⤢ 55 x 90 mm

🗋 Neenah Laid Duplex Natural White/Pepper Moss 324gsm

🖊 PMS 419 U

☀ Gluing, Folding

Bracket is a publication that catches everything in between - ideas, processes and voices that are yet to be discovered and appreciated. Like human relationships which require time and effort to build, the Bracket card invite you to use a little bit of strength to find the editor's contact details 'bracketed' in between the frames.

132

SPECIFICATIONS

⤢ 50.8 x 88.9 mm

🗋 Stainless Steel 200 Micron thick

🖊 -

☀ Etching, Laser-cut

Fork, knife and spoon would be the basic implements for preparing, serving and particularly eating food in Western culture, so the detachable silver cutlery set were there to tell who Mark Ramadan is and what his blog is about. The food service critic's card was partially inspired by the world-famous Kevin Mitnick's lock pick business card. The information security consultant was once a most-wanted computer criminal in the United States.

133

SPECIFICATIONS

- ⤢ 85 x 55 mm
- 🗎 Fedrigoni Century Cottone Wowe Ivory Uncoated 180gsm, M-Real Tauro White Uncoated 150gsm
- ✎ CMYK
- ✳ Laser-cut, Black cotton sewing thread

Serving as an easy and convenient portfolio to hold the different artworks of Nello Russo and Anna Follo, aka Mr and Ms SO, this card presents a new editorial project by the duo. For a lighthearted introduction, the couple's first release was a thaumatrope of Mr and Ms SO. They would look at each other and utter the word "SO" when the strings are twirled quickly enough.

134

SPECIFICATIONS

- ⤢ 85.6 x 54 mm
- 🗎 Recycled plastic
- ✎ 1 Spot colour (Permanent ink)
- ✳ Screenprint

A fresh, green plant would best describe Wieck as 'another bloomin' designer', so he made himself a card that carries little seeds inside. The card works like a miniature houseplant - just dip the foot of the card in water for four days and you would be expecting the seeds to sprout. An alfalfa or cress would eventually protrude and grow into the hair of the smiling face.

135

SPECIFICATIONS

- ⤢ 88.9 x 50.8 mm
- 🗎 14pt C2S Uncoated 300gsm
- ✎ CMYK
- ✳ -

Highlighting his personal preference for type treatment, Huynh gives his card an additional function with one side of his card turned into a 'typographic cheat sheet'. The letters were set in Feijoa.

136

SPECIFICATIONS

- ⤢ 85 x 53 mm
- 🗎 White Card 250gsm
- ✎ 4 versions: PMS 122 M, 344 M, 629 M, 693 M
- ✳ Flocking, Die-cut

Dogotel is a luxury pet service provider in Hong Kong, and a new set of communication tools was designed to promote their excellence in providing the best accommodation, training and grooming services for your pet dogs. A simple but loving impression was intended with a corner of the coloured stock cut in the shape of a doggie's paw.

137

SPECIFICATIONS

- ⤢ 55 x 85 mm
- 🗎 Tom & Otto Silk 300gsm
- ✎ CMYK
- ✳ Spot UV

Dutchtub by Floris Schoonderbeek is a mobile glass fibre tub that makes hot bath and barbecue possible at any time and anywhere you go, especially outdoor. Designed as the base of the brand's identity, the logo pieces together a whole new Dutchtub-world with landscape elements you could enjoy around the portable bowl.

138

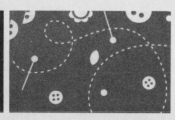

SPECIFICATIONS

- ⤢ 55 x 88 mm
- 🗎 9lives Offset 300gsm
- ✎ CMYK
- ✳ Vegetable oil based inks

Textile artist and maker, Claire Wellesley-Smith, aka Clarabella, is proficient in stitching innovative textile crafts and wearable pieces by reusing and re-dyeing vintage materials or used clothes and blankets. The Clarabella stationery echoes the maker's environmentally-friendly principles, with vegetable-oil-based inks and recycled paper and board in use.

139

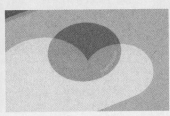

SPECIFICATIONS

- 85 x 55 mm
- Cairn Board 2000 Micron
- PMS White, 312 U
- Screenprint

The client's brief was a cool, contemporary and clean brand identity, which agrees with Pretty Green's friendly and welcoming approach to all projects and clients. The resulting identity is a beautifully simple and friendly one that brings light, attention and, more importantly, life to everyone. There's no set way to apply the badges, but they constitute a part to the memorable experience and tactility to printed matters.

140

SPECIFICATIONS

- 85 x 55 mm
- UPM Maxi Satin Coated 300gsm, UPM Maxi Offset Uncoated 100gsm
- CMYK
- Lamination, UV varnish, Bonding

Started off as the most playful hair studio in town, OZ hair is now inviting their clients to create their own crazy hair styles with their business cards. Could be a little too wavy or fluffy, but you should learn to manage them right away.

141

SPECIFICATIONS

- 89 x 50 mm
- Mohawk Superfine 240gsm
- CMYK
- Die-cut

Leaving an opening on the bald-headed illustration, this mono-colour card for hairstylist and makeup artist Yuka Suzuki can be customised by bobby pins as the hair. It could be your mini-hairstyling kit when you need to hold your hair in place!

142

SPECIFICATIONS

- 55 x 85 mm
- Offset Paper 300gsm
- CMYK
- Hand stamp with fluorescent ink

It has come to a time for the innovative Frankfurt duo to design for themselves. Imposing their very unconventional approaches to graphic design, a flexible identity was playfully realised with the use of stamps and neon inks. Business cards, letters and everything else are handmade and appears one of a kind.

143

SPECIFICATIONS

- 45 x 85 mm
- Mate Illustration White Paper 350gsm, Black Paper 350gsm
- CMYK, Mate/Brilliant Gold, Mate/Brilliant Silver, Iridicent Silver
- Foil block

One simple layout with nine appearances resulting from nine different stamping and foils defines what Playful does - variety. Pablo Alfieri's work is characterised by the chaos and order of structures, colour impacts, digital graphics and his constant search of simplicity in presenting geometrics shapes in design.

144

SPECIFICATIONS

- 90 x 55 mm
- Art Card 350gsm
- CMYK, PMS Black
- Gloss varnish

Also as artworks for Atomic Attack's office space décor, each card presents the founders-and-owners' portrait in a cool abstract style. Using illustration and elements that represent their love for self expression, illustration, toy and product making, the cards manifest that the design studio's works are more like a piece of art to admire.

SPECIFICATIONS

- ⤢ 90 x 60 mm
- 📄 Sarriópapel Supralbor Blanco 315gsm
- ✏ CMYK
- ✴ Spot UV, Varnish

OCU is an insurance brokerage that offers personalised insurance services to fit customers' respective needs. The business cards and stationery are made to remind clients how dangers exist everywhere and every day in a humorous but not too exaggerated way.

SPECIFICATIONS

- ⤢ 60 x 80 mm
- 📄 Sarriópapel Montana Extra Uncoated 300gsm
- ✏ CMYK
- ✴ -

Following Jorge Virgós' slogan 'for brands with soul', experienced Jorge Virgós stepped out the the creative world of advertising to offer his creative talent to projects that need a very personal approach. His business is all about changes and challenges. This only apparent chaos is symbolised by puffs of colourful mess.

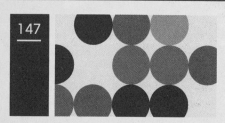

SPECIFICATIONS

- ⤢ 80 x 60 mm
- 📄 Sarriópapel Ensogloss 270gsm
- ✏ CMYK
- ✴ Varnish

POK is a networking service that allows a broad net of individuals to share mobile phone contents such as pictures, videos, blogs, contacts, etc. The cute, colourful dots represent the POK community that is constantly changing and energetic. With no specific logotype, POK's identity is in constant movement that varies with application and impress with a different pattern.

SPECIFICATIONS

- ⤢ 27.9 x 70.1 mm
- 📄 White Card Stock 80gsm
- ✏ CMYK
- ✴ Matt lamination

Launched to connect and engage the design community with dynamic and contemporary trends, OK Great is also a motivational tool for the team of designers, writers and artists to keep their mind fresh. With colour combinations renewing at the blog's head whenever you refresh the page, alternative rainbow stripes are also applied on the cards to accommodate the notion of variation in a concise and memorable way.

SPECIFICATIONS

- ⤢ 85 x 55 mm
- 📄 Matt Recycled Paper 250gsm
- ✏ CMYK
- ✴ -

Amsterdam-based Hanneke Beukers offers full project management and production service ranging from birthday parties to fashion shows. Beukers was represented a range of abstract icons combining the forms of Beukers' initials 'H' and 'B'.

SPECIFICATIONS

- ⤢ 88.9 x 50.8 mm
- 📄 Neenah Starwhite 460gsm
- ✏ CMYK
- ✴ -

Recognising itself as a new neighbourhood meat market that serves quality meats with old-school wits, The Chop Shop identity displays a mixed collection of retro types, primal cut diagrams and complimentary remarks about the shop's butchery to override its relatively young history. The idea of excellence continues with the featuring of rosettes and ribbon bars reminiscent of celebrations and awards.

151

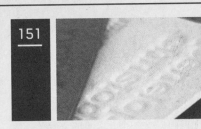

SPECIFICATIONS

⬀ 50 x 80 mm (Card),
30mm in diameter (Sticker)

▢ 3 versions: Coloured
Recycled Cardboard 8520gsm
(Card), Mat Vinyl (Sticker)

✎ PMS 292 C, 877 C, 1905 C
(Sticker)

✳ Blind deboss (Card)

Dedicated to photographing natural moments
or unique beauty for commercial purposes
or personal interest, Greek photographer,
Penelope Christodoulidi, was looking for an
eco-friendly yet aesthetically satisfac-
tory business card to represent herself.
The thick recycled cardboards, left from a
previous project, were intended with concise
information and adorned with stickers at the
back for a clean and approachable look.

152

SPECIFICATIONS

⬀ 55 x 85 mm

▢ Colourplan Natural 350gsm

✎ PMS 7505, 359

✳ Die-cut

'Hoa' is Vietnamese for 'blossoming flower',
and a new identity has been developed along
with the new unified space of Viet Hoa Cafe
and Bar, with Hoa's logo mark visible everywhere in a soft and earthy palette like
the sky and water in their home country. The
business card is combined with loyalty card,
where patrons collect stamps in return for
dinner discounts.

153

SPECIFICATIONS

⬀ 55 x 85 mm

▢ Dalton Paper Drink
Coaster Board 280gsm

✎ PMS Black

✳ -

Some think white collars would only grab a
coffee and go during their coffee breaks,
but Good Co. thinks they might indeed engage
the corporate executives as a 'Good Company
with Good Coffee'. The strong black-and-
white style and humourous dialogues were
imposed to break the usual code of coffee
environments in a casual yet relevant way.

154

SPECIFICATIONS

⬀ 82.6 x 57.2 mm

▢ Crane Kid Finish 264.95gsm

✎ PMS Black U

✳ Letterpress

Perky Bros was first established as a trans-
fer and storage company by Daniel Jefferson
Perky and brother, Albin in 1883 and, this
time around, by young Jefferson Perky, who
rebuilt the name with a design direction in
2009. Hefty letterpressed cards and thank
you notes dressed in the quality of tradi-
tions, and perforated labels to communicate
the resourcefulness of the shop today, as
labels and tapes.

155

SPECIFICATIONS

⬀ 85 x 55 mm

▢ GF Smith Colourplan 350gsm

✎ PMS Black U

✳ -

Morton & Peplow is a Munich delicatessen
that specialises in British cuisine. The
identity combines two icons of Britishness -
the bowler hat and the domed silver service
platter - to create a mark that evokes a
sense of heritage and style. A candy colour
palette and classic typography serve to
continue this quintessentially British feel,
tipping its hat to a lost era of elegant
simplicity.

156

SPECIFICATIONS

⬀ 54 x 85 mm (Closed)

▢ Teton Warm White 118gsm

✎ Custom red

✳ Emboss, Gluing, Folding

With the intent to continue learning and
push the boundaries of creation, a collaborative studio, comprising Matthew
Schneider of Carefully Considered, Hafez
Janssens of FEZ and Nessim Higson of IAAH,
was brought together to this 'TENT' or
'10NT' to pursue unrealised projects that
could otherwise be left untounched. Take a
peek into their tents and you will find 'new
ideas in design'.

157

SPECIFICATIONS

- ⤢ 38.1 x 88.9 mm (Card),
  90.6 x 25.4 mm (Sticker)
- ◻ Powder Coated Steel (Card),
  Mohawk Superfine Ultrawhite
  Smooth 60lb Cover (Sticker)
- ✎ PMS 021, 185, 389, 549,
  559, 637
- ✳ Letterpress

Furniture design and manufacturing company Bludot aims to bring good designs to as many as they can, and they have accomplished it by producing desirable and practical products at distinctively affordable prices. With the use of the very personalised powder-coated steels, Bludot's business cards communicate the brand's aesthetics in four colours to choose from. The paper pieces are offset and letterpressed by Studio on Fire.

158

SPECIFICATIONS

- ⤢ 50.8 x 88.9 mm
- ◻ Various recycled paper
- ✎
- ✳ Hand stamp with regular
  stamp pad (7 Colours)

JAM is a community-based art initiative conceived by Nova Scotia-based artist Julie Adamson Miller. Since JAM incorporates many different practices and people, the visual identity had to reflect diversity and positivity. Rubber stamps were chosen as a playful and cost-effective means of printing, allowing almost any material to be JAM's communication platform.

159

SPECIFICATIONS

- ⤢ 55 x 90 mm
- ◻ Toku A Cushion 1mm
- ✎ 2 PMS
- ✳ -

CHICKEN PECKER is a specialty store in Hokkaido, Japan. With promises in serving quality hamburgers and fried chicken assured by organic farming and strict food processing supervision, the identity runs in parallel with its vision to bring an authentic taste of fresh and healthy chickens in the colours of lush greenery and natural kraft paper. The concept was a sign in the countryside.

160

SPECIFICATIONS

- ⤢ 55 x 85 mm
- ◻ Revive Uncoated 325gsm
- ✎ PMS 116 U, 130 U, 145 U,
  1595 U, Warm Grey 10 U
- ✳ Emboss (Wallet)

Hive is a small hair and beauty salon chain in London. The logo was created to recall the busy scenes at the salon place with the shape of honey combs in warm yet vivid orange throughout. The individual letters are arranged in different combinations. Single spot colours and embossing were used.

161

SPECIFICATIONS

- ⤢ 85 x 55 mm
- ◻ Revive 100 Uncoated 325gsm
- ✎ CMYK
- ✳ -

Identity for a children's animation artist. The letters of the logo change randomly, with an unusual navigation on the website opening all content within in a section at the same time.

162

SPECIFICATIONS

- ⤢ 55 x 85 mm
- ◻ Revive Uncoated 325gsm
- ✎ PMS Black 3 U, 368 U
- ✳ -

'Tea' is a chain of tea shops, comprising an online shop, a retail shop at a popular tourist spot in London and wholesale services for food services. Coordinating the simple British love affair with tea, a clean typographic design was applied to tea's logo, recognised by the little tea leaf on the letter 't'. A colour scheme is applied on tea packaging as a friendly index to categorise the different type of teas.

163

SPECIFICATIONS

⬈ 90 x 38 mm

🗋 Daltons Threads 350gsm

🖊 PMS 485 U, 9184 U

✳ -

Aviary is a small fashion boutique targeting middle-aged female local shoppers and passing commuters from Melbourne on their weekend country solstice. The vintage bird illustrations are the natural visuals of the store's name. An Asian undertone is reflective of the furniture style which adorns the store fit-out.

164

SPECIFICATIONS

⬈ 55 x 85 mm

🗋 Starwhite Smooth White 352gsm

🖊 CMYK

✳ Deboss

Founder of Pixel Flix has specifically request to shun film-related clichés in the identity and now his affability and liveliness is pervading the identity in a trustworthy sense. The package is set to explore the editing process, from the unorganised pieces to a comprehensive result, just like the messy strokes that gradually restored to spell 'PIXELFLIX'. The business card contains two layers of card stock for additional strength.

165

SPECIFICATIONS

⬈ 55 x 85 mm

🗋 Conqueror CX22 Oyster 320gsm

🖊 PMS Black U, 032 U, 877 U, 2945 U, 3385 U

✳ -

Coming in a variation of type design based on a art-deco inspired modular system, TESS represents notable models such as Naomi Campbell and Erin O'Connor in the UK. The TESS-marks also appear on model's portfolio frames and print applications, as well as the agency's website.

INDEX

THANK YOU

We would like to thank all the designers and companies. This project would not have been accomplished without their significant contribution to the compilation of this book. We would also like to express our gratitude to all the producers for their invaluable assistance throughout this entire proposal. The successful completion also owes a great deal to many professionals in the creative industry who have given us precious insights and comments. We would also like to extend thanks to the many others whose names are not credited but have made specific input and continuous support the whole time.

FUTURE EDITIONS

If you would like to contribute to the next edition of Victionary, please email us your details to submit@victionary.com